THE JEWEL IN THE LOTUS

GRACE COOKE
1892–1979

The Golden Key (1929)
Plumed Serpent (1942)
The Shining Presence (1946)
The Open Door (1946)
Meditation (1955)
The New Mediumship (1965)
The Illumined Ones (1966)
The Light in Britain (*with Ivan Cooke*, 1971)
The Jewel in the Lotus (1973)
Sun Men of the Americas (1975)

The first four of the above titles are out of print

THE JEWEL IN
THE LOTUS

GRACE COOKE

THE WHITE EAGLE PUBLISHING TRUST

LISS · HAMPSHIRE · ENGLAND

First published October 1973
Reprinted May 1977
Reprinted February 1980
Reprinted March 1985 (first paperback edition)
Reprinted May 1987
Reprinted March 1992

ISBN: 0-85487-067-9

Printed in Great Britain by
WILLIAM CLOWES LIMITED, BECCLES AND LONDON

CONTENTS

FOREWORD

Meditation, popular though it is today, is no new art invented by modern man desperately looking for a way out of his dilemma; for saints and mystics of every age have sought knowledge of God and of their own inner being through its practice. They have known the inexpressible happiness—ecstasy is hardly too strong a word—which the aspirant can experience through deep meditation, the natural unfoldment of the spiritual power within the heart. They have known the inner strength and power to accomplish it can bestow, the stronghold of deep peace it can create in the soul. Whole new worlds of experience open up for the aspirant who can find the 'way in' through creative meditation. A new awareness can come to him, a new power to serve God and man.

Grace Cooke, the author of this book, is the founder and leader of the White Eagle Lodge, and well known and loved as the dedicated instrument through whom the White Eagle teaching has been given to the world. She has been teaching students the art of creative meditation for more than thirty years and during that time has witnessed the effect on the lives of those who have been thus enabled to draw nearer to the Source of their being.

Her first book on meditation, published in 1955, has been reprinted many times since then, so popular has it proved. It is, in a sense, an introduction to the subject. In this, her second book on meditation, she covers new ground and points a clear path into inner worlds; and by drawing on students' own accounts she gives the key to interpretation of the experiences which come during the hours of meditation. These interpretations are wonderfully illuminating, and simply to read the book, with the wealth of sound teaching it contains, is to feel lifted out of the confusion of earth into the light.

The Jewel in the Lotus is sent out with the earnest prayer that for many, many readers it may prove to be the key to their release from the fetters of the earth and the lower mind; that through its pages they may learn to rise as White Eagle so beautifully puts it into 'the golden world of God.'

Y. G. H.

1973

THE LAKE OF PEACE

Arise out of yourself,
Let go the garment of the body:
Seek the place of healing silence and tranquillity,
Seek the lake of peace within,
Calm and tideless.
Let the boat of the mind glide slowly from its
    moorings
(Leave the turbulent, restless river)
Past the soft green fingers of the rushes,
Into the lake's cool silver,
Quiet rippling at the prow.
Here the unruffled heart must wait.
Wait not impatiently for the long-sought action,
The eager self outstretched to grasp
And to hold tightly.
Wait gently—as the water waits
For the cool touch of light upon its moving stillness,
For the pulse of the evening air—
Steadily beating.
There is calm here and awareness of nature,
So be tranquil and aware of God.
Though the hand of time is still closed to your
    desires,
Let go desire for it is the measure of your
    uncertainty,
Your lack of faith.
By the clear light of aspiration
You shall see:
You shall see there is peace in acceptance
That His will may be done.
Rest in the timeless centre of your being,
The dwelling place of wisdom.
When you are ready
The appointed hour shall come.   T.D.

I

MAN'S ADVENTURE INTO A NEW WORLD

I have memories of a time ages back when I was living among the mountains. Looking up to the mountain peaks piercing the mists, I thought what fun it would be to fly like a bird up through those mists to the sun beyond. As the sun grew stronger, it gradually penetrated the mists which began to disperse, revealing, as they rolled away, peak after peak of a vast range.

White Eagle himself has often used the simile of mountain ranges to describe the process of spiritual unfoldment; as one peak is attained, another higher peak is revealed, then another and another, until the whole range opens up before the climber. Indeed the same is true of all the experiences of life itself: as soon as one problem is solved you are faced with another. This may sound somewhat discouraging, but as you proceed with your climb it becomes a delightful adventure, leading you on and up into a golden spirit world. This is why White Eagle says to us on earth, 'Keep on keeping on.' However, the desire to climb into the beauty and clean air of the sunlit country beyond is the first step to attainment. If we use our creative power and imagine ourselves in the world above and beyond the mists, we can find ourselves in a beautiful garden where we can walk at will, wandering down 'imaginary' green paths of perfectly cut turf, bordered with tiny flowering plants of many colours. The turfed path leads towards a lake surrounded by hills. The water of the lake looks so clear and blue that one longs to plunge into it and feel its healing coolness. We smell the sweet freshness of the water and feel its caressing touch; we listen to the harmonious sound like music as it laps the shore of the lake. The water seems to be part of us and we of it. Sister water, we love you!

We notice that the pebbles on the shore, washed by the clear water and gleaming in the sunlight, are like brightly coloured jewels. How lovely, we think, is the sight of these rainbow colours which grow in intensity as we gaze, rejoicing in nature's beauty.

Now we see a narrow grass path leading up the hillside. It looks inviting, so we wander up it. As we walk, we can hear the lark's song, far above us; but beyond this, and the quiet lapping at the water's edge, there is a deep deep stillness and silence. And beneath the stillness there is a sound. Is it music? Or the murmur of voices? It is a gentle hum, almost like a swarm of bees. As we listen it grows a little louder, and the vibration seems to sound through our bodies. We feel exhilarated by it and, as it grows louder still, we are caught up in it and become intoxicated by its power. It is the great AUM that we hear. . . . It begins as a gentle breeze, and slowly develops into a mighty rushing wind; with its coming we are caught up off the ground and seem to be carried on and up, as on wings, up into unimaginable sunlight. . . .

Again we find ourselves by the side of a small lake or pool, rectangular in shape, and around it is a still group of people seated in the lotus position, looking into a lotus flower or pure white lily. Gazing into its centre we see the golden stamens and, nestling in them, a sparkling jewel. We are entranced by its scintillating beauty, but even more than this we sense deep within ourselves a purity and holiness impossible to put into words. Let us be still, and know God. . . .

The mind of earth is stilled, it is in abeyance . . . we have mastered the clamour of mind and body and have entered into a heavenly consciousness. We realise our at-one-ment with nature, with Mother Earth, with the great Mother of all form, the creative love which moulds the white ether into every form of life there is. Once again we become aware of the group of elder brothers, sainted ones, who have found, through life's experience, the reality within the centre or heart of life, the centre or heart of man, which we are told is the Christ Spirit.

Through suffering and trial they have found the way to eternal life. This Christ Spirit is the shining jewel we see in the heart of the lily, the jewel within the lotus, the jewel within our own heart.

II

THE PURPOSE OF MEDITATION

In the profound silence of the soul, when all thoughts of the earth are stilled, the turbulent emotions subdued, and the mind set on thoughts of the heaven world, the divinity dwelling in the soul, the inner light of the Christ Spirit, begins to stir . . . an inner feeling, deep within ourselves, which brings us closer to God. This feeling lies beneath all thought; it is an awareness of an enfolding love, a strengthening and upholding power, deep within our own being and linking our spirit with the cosmic life. We cannot *think* our way to this centre of truth, we can only *feel* it or realise it. In the profound silence, when thought is still and the turbulent emotions and egotism of the personality are subdued, it is then that we reach the centre of truth and find God.

The mind demands proof of spiritual things; it wants a demonstration of the reality of life after death. It wants to know how spiritual law works, and what the superphysical life is like. But the answers to these questions will not come through a mental process; they will be revealed to man's inmost spirit in moments of deep meditation.

White Eagle reminds us of the danger of putting too much emphasis on the mind, because, he says, the mind can destroy. 'The mind can kill all beauty, and often kills truth and your own happiness; it can destroy your health. But the divine spirit, which is gentle and compassionate love, brings life and health, beauty and harmony. To achieve perfect balance the mind must be governed and used by the spirit, which is pure and divine love. The mind is an unruly horse. Your spirit is not unruly because it is of God and is all truth; and your spirit must master that unruly steed. The mind can be overruled by the activity of the brain, which is of earth; but spirit, pure spirit is ever true to God and is expressed in the simple love in your heart—the love which heals.'

The ancient brethren, men and women who earnestly sought for a deeper understanding of God, withdrew for a time from the outer life, the world of everyday, and lived within a community of kindred souls in order to seek, through meditation and the contemplative way of life, the secrets of God and the universe. These monastic settlements or brotherhoods have existed throughout the ages and in all countries, both in the east and in the west, and were not confined to orthodoxy nor the Christian Church.

White Eagle, in his communication from the spirit life, has spoken of the White Brotherhood in the remote past in South America, of which he says he was a brother. The illumined ones in his day were known as Plumed Serpents and were identified by the crown of soft plumes round the head. These head-dresses symbolised the white radiance around the head of initiates of the order of the Great White Light. The radiance or the aura which surrounds the head of a saint, as so frequently depicted by mediaeval artists, is really this same Light.

In the earliest times, before man became intellectually developed (and perhaps one could say intellectually arrogant), the guiding Light deep within his soul revealed to him divine laws which govern all life, knowledge of which helped him to live harmoniously and in communion with God. This ancient wisdom was lost as man became more deeply involved at the physical level, but pointers to these lost secrets of life were left by the ancient White Brotherhood, written on their stone temples, all over the earth. The origin of many of these temples remains a complete mystery, but their secrets can be uncovered when man finds the key—and this lies in his heart.

When a man experiences a state of true, deep meditation, he becomes absolutely convinced of the reality of the world of spirit, and of life beyond the grave. Whereas before he had to rely on others to describe these spirit worlds, he has now touched the centre of truth and can say with unshakeable conviction, 'I know this spiritual life is real.' This conviction increases with his own spiritual development so that he no longer needs physical proof of the spirit world and life after death. He *knows*.

In the early days of modern Spiritualism, physical manifestations from the spirit world convinced scientist and layman alike of the truth of life beyond death. The materialisation of the soul body after death, as demonstrated at that time, is really rather a clumsy way of proving the truth of the after life. What we are working for, and achieving, in meditation is the spiritualisation of matter rather than the materialisation of spirit. In meditation every individual soul can reach the source of truth and experience the reality of spirit for himself. With the development of man's intellect in this Aquarian Age, any material proof can easily be destroyed by the critical mind; but a conviction based on experience deep in the heart can never be shaken.

In my earlier book I have described how to meditate according to White Eagle's method and have outlined the purpose and value of meditation in everyday life. The book also contains readings designed to help raise the consciousness and lead the aspirant into higher worlds.

In this first section of the present book, I shall endeavour to show the way to achieve the purest possible contact with the spirit world through meditation. In doing so I am assuming that you have studied my first book, and are therefore conversant with our method. You will know that the first object of your meditation must always be aspiration towards God, the heavenly Father, and realisation of your at-one-ment with God and with all life. The brothers of old always concentrated their aspirations, prayer and meditations upon God, the heavenly Father. They conceived the heavenly Father as being the supreme and almighty Spirit over-ruling all life; but logically one cannot separate the Father from the Mother or from the Son in the worship of God, because all three aspects of created life are embodied in the one supreme Power which is all-good, all-truth.

This trinity is the basis of life at every level and through all planes of consciousness from the lowest to the most high. Moreover all forms of life are of the one spirit, all of one great family of God, the heavenly Father, the divine Mother, and the Son. This deep mystical truth of the trinity has as its symbol the triangle.

At the start of our meditation therefore it will help us if we imagine or picture a golden tri-angle or, it may be, a mountain peak bathed in the golden light of the sun, towards which we rise in worship and adoration of that supreme power in which we are embraced. We start our meditation at this point. It is essential at the very beginning to make this real and strong contact with that golden light on the mountain peak. Rise in consciousness into the light and concentrate upon the light, the sun. Imagine you are in the highest heights in the golden light; feel the presence and power and warmth of the life-force, the sun of God in your own heart. Dwell in this for quite a time, breathing deeply and slowly, realising as you do so that you are breathing in the sunlight of God, the golden life-force.

White Eagle says: 'In your meditation we direct you first of all to rise to the apex of the golden triangle and there meditate on the Great White Light or the Golden One, the Christos. As you go directly and earnestly to that point and focus your worship, your adoration, your consciousness in that universal and infinite Light, you must at the same time bring all your devotion, all your power to that one supreme point. This creates in you the perfectly straight line of light from the base of your spine to the crown of the head, like the mason's plumb line. Not only is your body straight, and the power rising straight up through your body, but all your concentration is on God, on what is good, what is lovely, what is beautiful, what is true, just and wise—the whole being is brought into poise, into straightness.'

We have also been told by White Eagle that sound plays an important part in meditation, and have been instructed by him to sound 'the Word.' What does he mean by this? In the first chapter of St. John's gospel we read: 'In the beginning was the Word and the Word was with God and the Word was God.' The Word was God, or good. God is good, God is love, God is wisdom. Because man's spirit is part of God, made in the image of God, all these attributes are in the human spirit, and can be developed by thought and aspiration, by good thought or God thought.

In ancient freemasonry the candidate was taught to apply the tools and the rules of operative masonry symbolically to his character and always to 'act on the square'—to be just, perfect and true in his relationship with his fellow craftsmen. If he lives in this way he creates on the higher levels of life a vibration, a sound, which, while inaudible to the physical ear, reverberates powerfully in the inner or soul world.

The sound by which we interpret this 'lost word' is contained in a mantram which advanced students learn. The complete mantram cannot be published in this book. But we can explain that at the sounding of each one of the syllables of the mantram there occurs a stimulation of cells in the brain attuned to different levels of consciousness, or spiritual spheres of life. As these cells become increasingly active, the power to create form and beauty increases. It is through these brain cells that inspiration is received by man from the higher spheres of ideation.

The first syllable of the mantram can be explained here, and it is a sound of which the aspirant can become aware in the deep deep silence of the inner self or soul. Let us imagine that we are far removed from the noise of the market place, alone on a remote mountain peak and we hear in the silence of eternity a murmur, a sound, like the beat of waves on the shore, or the wind across the moorland. We hear the hum of all life. The closest we can get to inter-

preting that hum of life is the drawn out
O-o-o-mmm. In the beginning was sound—the
Word, and the Word was God—AUM.

Therefore in the beginning of meditation we
seek to hear the Word of God in the silence. We
sound the Word ... AUM ... which, reverberating throughout the whole being, creates
a powerful vibration. Be still, and know God.
Be still, and know that I AM God. The I AM
deep, deep within, the spirit—God. This is the
jewel within the lotus of the heart, and White
Eagle calls it the Christ Light or the jewel of
Christ, the Son of God.

White Eagle says: 'We are trying to help you
to realise this pure truth in the silence of your
own heart. We are trying to help you to realise
the divine presence ... God in you, God in all
creation. God is and ever has been. From the
heart of God all creatures have been born.
God animates all matter and causes it first to
become, then to grow and to evolve.

'The Word was sound, vibration, and the
vibration created by the Word started life in
form. The scriptures of the world all contain
this same truth, they all tell of the Word, the
sound, the vibration, the activity of the atom
which created form or life on the earth.
This is the beginning of life in the universe;
then when mortal life has run its course, there
comes a turning inward, a withdrawal from
that outer manifestation.

'When man has become cognisant of this
divine law, and of this essence, God, in the

heart and centre both of his own being and of the whole universe, then he realises that he is not separate but part of the whole, and part of God, and God is in him; thus slowly he merges into this greater consciousness, into the *all*-ness of life.

'At this stage brotherhood of the spirit, brotherhood of all life, is realised by man. When, in the deep silence, man knows God, he knows all.'

Some of my students have described the communion they have felt with the heavenly Father:*

> ▓ As we ascended the golden mountain peak, I felt caught up in a great triangle of pulsating life, aspiring upwards—up, up, up I went—and then at the very peak, a flood of spiritual ecstasy went through me as a triangle of light descended from heaven and a perfect six-pointed star was formed. This blazing star, just pulsated with light, which was sent out all over the world. The wonderful thing was that I was right in IT.

> ▓ I visualised the upward triangle, and then the downward triangle, and the feeling to me was beyond any words to convey; whereas in previous classes I have found it so

* *Throughout the book, students' meditations will appear indented and marked* ▓ *to distinguish them from the main text.*

difficult to co-ordinate the breathing, intoning and visualisation, this time it was so amazing to me to see the light of the triangle as I breathed in, and then, sounding the AUM, well, it seemed as if I was rising, rising in Light. It was as if I was held in the living pulsating Light; all blessing and peace came as if my very soul was enfolded in eternity.

I had the feeling of absolute stillness and silence and was quite alone except it seemed for the presence of God. I was so aware of this presence and anxious to become more and more aware that as part of His creation I was also part of Him. Then faint, faint sounds were all around and I was conscious of LIFE —the rustle of the wind, the trickle of water, the awakening of birds and the whole sky became suffused with the glorious colours of the dawn—pink, gold, jade green, mauve, then violet, then orange and at that moment the sun appeared over the opposite mountain peak; it grew bigger and bigger and more brilliant until it was too dazzling and I closed my eyes.

You instructed us to visualise a golden disc while we listened to the heavenly music. As I gazed upon this golden disc which just filled the room, it glowed even more with soft golden light which became larger and larger as it gradually enfolded us all. This disc of golden light became more and more beautiful and we were raised up, and then there formed a golden temple with beautiful pillars all in circular form. Then this golden disc became the floor and foundation of a glorious circular temple, and we were all kneeling round in a circle. Then there appeared a most heavenly Form. I could not see His presence plainly. It was His aura which was all light—so gentle, so still yet all love flowed out to us all. It is beyond words to convey as each one sees Him–Her according to their awareness and understanding. The very atmosphere and aura enfolded one in peace, and as I came to as the music ceased there appeared the most perfect pure white rose. It was not quite opened but oh! so beautiful in its simplicity.

All these meditations embody the intense happiness the aspirant feels at the moment of conscious communion with God the heavenly Father. I have already explained that this aspiration towards God must be the first object of your meditation. The beautiful opening white rose described in the last account could symbolise the unfolding spirit of the student.

III

THE CREATIVE IMAGINATION

In the previous chapter we have found that sounding the Word can stimulate certain cells in the brain to become receptive to impressions from higher levels of thought, or from divine spirit. The next step is to bring into operation the higher, subliminal mind, and use the gift of imagination to create form and beauty in the inner world. You must develop the power to visualise or create the perfect image in the inner world. The power of pure heavenly imagination must be cultivated, for this is the only way for man to see for himself the life which is lived in the heavenly world to which he is aspiring.

It is important to distinguish clearly between fancy, and imagination or creative imagery. One can fancy all kinds of evil and negative things happening in the world or to one's friends and acquaintances, but this is not true imagination, it is morbid thinking. The student must learn to break through the bondage of the material and earthly mind, which always fills the soul with doubts, fears and criticism, and particularly with the feeling that creative imagination is all just fancy or make believe.

The real meaning of spiritual imagination is the creation in the higher or subliminal mind of a language or a form which expresses pure beauty, pure goodness and pure Christ Love.

White Eagle says: 'In your meditations you are told first of all to rise into the heights, because by so doing you withdraw from the clamour of the thought forms and all the mists which gather around you at the material level of life. So first of all you are taken right up into the heights, to the golden apex of the mountain, where you become absorbed in a glorious heavenly light. At this moment you touch the true light, and by so doing begin to create and develop a solar body, a body of light. If you do nothing else during your meditations but become enabled for a few moments to bask in that pure and true light, you are still doing very well. Later on you will be told to use your higher mind, the mind of God, the divine creative mind, which also has to be developed and which can become a very powerful instrument. You will be told to create a picture with your higher mind, to create form.

'We want you to understand that man can create infinite beauty because the divine mind in him can manipulate the white ether. People who do not understand will think this is all imagination and that nothing created in this way is real. But the ether is a very real substance, more real than physical matter, and the higher or divine mind in you can mould that sensitive ether into living form.

'Many people have an intense appreciation of the beauties of the kingdom of nature, where the infinite love of the Creator is revealed; joy comes to man's heart through the beauty of the sky, the colour and form created by the clouds, the song of the birds and the perfume of flowers, the glory of the rolling seas and the colour reflected in the water. Many people can recognise and enjoy these beauties, but they cannot get beyond what the physical eyes are seeing. Yet there are some who are able to use their feeling, and as they stand lost in wonder before some scene of natural beauty, through imagination they can feel the glorious presence of God beyond or within the physical form. When listening to music they can respond to sound reverberating through the universe, quite beyond the physical sound. Through imagination a man accustomed to express his soul in words is able to touch worlds remote from this and to convey to others the vision vouchsafed to his higher mind and spirit.

'It is important that we all recognise the value of imagination, because most people are so afraid of being deceived that they draw a heavy curtain between themselves and the real world of spirit. We tell you most earnestly that true and real imagination is the doorway into the etheric world, into the higher mental world and beyond that, into the celestial or heavenly world, and even beyond again into the cosmic world. You will never find what your soul seeks through reading books, unless your spirit is awakened, or quickened. The spirit is supreme; the spirit is of God and is God; and man, if he will become simple as a child, can enter the kingdom of heaven through pure spirit.

'Man's spirit is not his mind, and his mind is not his brain—but pure spirit will use the higher mind of man, that mind which lies beneath the surface of the mind of earth.

'The higher mind is free from all earthly entanglements; it does not think in terms of money or possessions, nor is it concerned with material things. The higher mind is only concerned with the everlasting life of the cosmos. This is not to say, however, that the higher mind is indifferent to the lower levels of life. The more the higher mind develops, the greater the wisdom which comes into man's ordinary consciousness.

'When you meditate, if you are working correctly, you will be conscious only of more beautiful and harmonious conditions of life; these you will be able to see, to hear, to feel, to taste and to smell with your etheric senses. When meditating you are not only thinking or contemplating abstractly; with your higher mind you are creating a condition of life in which at that moment you are living and participating. Do understand this. You are being led step by step along the path into those higher worlds of harmony and peace, truth and wisdom. But it is not an abstract condition; it is a world of form in which you are living during your meditation.

'Your leader may give you a picture to imagine or think about; perhaps lovely mountain peaks, and one in particular which is capped with the golden light, and by certain ritual helps you to rise until you are in a higher state of consciousness on the mountain peaks or in the infinite and eternal garden. Through the ritual used you are bringing into operation a super-conscious mind, a mind which is superior to all normal, ordinary thought.

'This is the mind which is used in meditation, and the description given to you of that heaven world, which your higher mind or superior mind takes up, becomes for you a real world during your meditation. If what you are seeing and experiencing is beautiful and inspiring, and makes you feel at peace with your fellow beings and all life, then surely that must be good, and an aspect of life to be encouraged and developed. You need not fear intrusion or darkness, for if the thought and aspirations are pure, the aspirant is always protected by the power of God, which is all good, all love.

'It is said that man has to be practical on the physical plane and that he cannot be practical while he is thinking of spiritual things. We must not become dreamy, the mind of earth tells us; we must not be carried away by illusion or we will be confused and useless in everyday life. Now this is entirely wrong. If man, through true and correct meditation, is entering into a higher state of consciousness and becoming aware of worlds unknown to him in his state of mental and spiritual imprisonment, then surely such a man is on the path to becoming what we can only describe as a man made perfect in the Christ Spirit.

'You ask, how can we tell the difference between true imagination and mere fancy or fantasy? True imagination comes as the result of the reaction on the brain of higher vibrations which have been set in motion by your sincere aspiration and prayer. You can think all kinds of unworthy and foolish thoughts with your lower mind, but when you have touched that power and golden light at the apex of the mountain, as we have described, you are suffused with that God power, and that affects not only your higher mind but your brain, so that you are able to create, by the power of God, the form described to you to help you to break through into the world of spirit. This is why we always guide you first of all to go right up to the highest heights, to the great white and golden Spirit, and there make your contact. Then you can give yourself to the unfolding vision, which will carry you on beyond your leader's guidance.'

IV

THE INFINITE AND ETERNAL GARDEN AND THE DIVINE MOTHER

In White Eagle's method of leading us into meditation, after we have made that initial contact in the golden light at the apex of the mountain, he instructs us to use the creative imagination in order to visualise in the soul world a most perfect and beautiful garden— what he calls 'the infinite and eternal garden.'

In creating a garden in the inner worlds we have a wide choice of season and setting. For instance, it may be spring-time in our garden, or high summer with all its rich colour and life; we might see the garden set in a perfect land-scape with majestic trees, flowering shrubs and herbaceous borders; or with rock gardens and a running brook of pure clear water through which can be seen stones like jewels, and fish of different colours; there may be smooth green lawns, or a blue lake. In these surroundings we are able to use our creative imagination to develop our spiritual senses. As we observe the light and life in all the beautiful form, we develop our spiritual sense of sight; and our spiritual sense of sound as we listen to the song of birds, the trickle of water in the brooks and waterfalls, the music of the gentle wind in the trees. We can develop our spiritual sense of smell as we inhale the pungent freshness of the earth and the subtle perfumes of the variety of flowers, some of which may be unknown to us on earth. We develop too our spiritual sense of taste as in imagination we try the fruit from bush, tree and vine, and cup our hands to sip the fresh sweet water; our sense of touch as our hands are immersed in that cool water, or laid upon the living stones which edge the lily pool.

In this garden we feel the presence of the divine Mother—truly the spirit of motherhood. And it is the realisation of this all-enfolding love, compassion and tenderness that makes the deepest and most lasting impression upon us as we meditate in the infinite and eternal garden.

In the western world, reference to the divine Mother is assumed to be to Mary, mother of Jesus. But the ancients would say that the Mother, the great Mother Earth, was another aspect of God the Father, the two in one, the parents of humanity, and thus the picture of a dual deity emerges. If one thinks of the Father as the spiritual as well as the physical sun and the Mother as giving form to all life—the corn, the fruit, the trees, the flowers, the creatures— then one can see why the ancients worshipped God the Father as the Creator, the energy, and God the Mother, the womb in which the seed of life is nurtured by the warmth of the sun.

In the dawn of life souls were taught by angelic messengers to worship God as the Mother. To them the great Mother whom they adored represented the giver of life, the pre-server of life, who gave all the fruits of the earth for their sustenance. The great Mother was therefore worshipped and adored equally with the Father and when the people of earth can return to the worship of that beautiful Mother there will be a return to happiness.

White Eagle tells us that the form of divine Mother with her angels is always present watch-ing over the miracle of birth on the physical plane. She represents both the universal spirit of motherhood, working through the soul and body of the physical mother, and the human form of divine Mother which can be seen ministering at the birth.

The same thing happens at every so-called death. Many times have I been told from the spirit life that the departing soul being reborn into the world of spirit is met and cherished either by its own mother or a spirit mother. Thus the mother plays a most important part in ministering both at the entry of the soul into matter and at its departure.

The appearance of divine Mother is not in-frequent to those who know her. She comes as the spirit of the beautiful and perfect woman. She is woman made perfect, even as Christ is man made perfect. As you conceive the attributes and the qualities of the Christ in a man, so does the divine Mother manifest as a personality in the perfect form, beauty and attributes of a mother. To each nationality she appears as one of their own race. Therefore, to a European she will appear as such, very beautiful in face and form, clothed in the softest white flowing robes, with a cloak of heavenly madonna blue; to me her hair is golden, her eyes a deep blue. An aura of light comprising all the softest colours of the spectrum radiates from her, and a sweet subtle perfume of roses. She is beautiful beyond compare. She is universal spirit which takes the human form of a mother because it is the easiest way to come very close to all her children on earth, to help them, to comfort them in time of sorrow, bitterness or loneliness, and to add to their joy in times of happiness. Through her human–divine personality she reaches right down into the very depths of the human heart. We all yearn for a mother's love, a mother's understanding, and in the divine Mother we find the comfort and deep spiritual peace which is the culmination of life and happiness.

Some of the accounts of my students show how this sense of the divine Mother's love was conveyed to them in their meditations:

▨ I was in the spirit garden in the centre of which sat the great Mother surrounded by happy, active children, who came forward to greet us. One little child took my hand and asked, 'Would you like to see our rose garden?' and took me into a most beautiful garden, with roses of all colours and scents. She picked a bunch of rose-buds and gave them to me, spraying them with heavenly dew to help them to last longer. Then she took us to see the bird garden, full of the most lovely and brightest coloured birds. She said, 'My favourite one is that little plain grey-brown bird, because his is the most beautiful song of all. They are so tame that any one called by name will come and settle on your hands.' Then she told us, 'We had lots and lots of animals of all kinds in parts of the garden, but unless you are used to them I will not show them to you, as you might feel afraid. You see we are not afraid, as even the fiercest will come and lick our hands, or rub their noses on our faces.' Then she said, 'I will show you the loveliest of all our views—it is that very tall purple mountain you can see across the valley with its rippling stream. On top of it is a temple of worship where you can see, inside its centre, the shining form of our Master, Jesus Christ; I am going to try to climb that mountain when I am older. But Jesus comes to visit us here often.'

From my experience this is a perfectly true meditation of a young mother, as well as a lover of the nature kingdom. It expresses humility and simplicity of the soul and a pure love for God and nature.

▦ I saw a very beautiful and spacious garden of lawns and flowers surrounded by magnificent trees. In the centre, by a pool of pure water, was seated the great Mother keeping watch over babies and children who had passed on prematurely. She rocked the babies quietly in her lap until they slept, and they were then taken by lovely white-winged angels and placed near scented flowers until they wakened. The older children were playing happily around her. Some had been given materials with which to create objects according to their abilities; others were splashing in the pool, delighting to feel sister water playing on their bodies, and sitting within brother sunshine to get dried. Others were helping the flower fairies create their blossoms and taking little bowls of different colours to them, with which to paint them. All were so happily employed, and not one thought of grasping anything for himself, as each felt he was part of the whole life of this beautiful garden and wanted to make it even more lovely. Then as the day wore on, the mother rose from her seat and called all the children round her. She led them into a shining temple, and at the golden altar stood the Lord Christ waiting to bless and greet each child as it knelt in loving gratitude, before being taken away by the winged angels. . . .

The mother was the guardian of the child,

the immature soul. The lesson from this meditation is that we are all just children learning to use the gifts of the Father–Mother God.

༄ I aspired then to the divine Mother, because I knew I was untrammelled by earth. Her temple was the universe and I was in her temple. I knew she was there, and had taken the form of a warm, loving mother, with a great welcoming heart. I became a little child and rested in her arms. I sat on her knee and looked about me and saw all creation at her feet. Then I turned to her and looked into her heart and it was the pink rose of love. I was the heart of the rose. 'Here in the garden of creation all things are perfect, are made perfect.' She told me to look down and I saw the stalk of the rose descending a long way into the dark. She said this was I. The rose was my higher self and would I like to see it blooming? I wanted to, but felt it was not yet time to do so completely. I was very happy in this golden/white/rose temple.

This illustrates the help given to the individual through the love of the divine Mother and her angels. We see here the awakening spiritual consciousness in the meditator and a growing understanding of the symbolism in mental and spiritual experience.

༄ I felt an awareness of the divine Motherhood, the very essence enfolded my soul and aura; it was part of my soul at this sacred moment so that I felt as if I held the Christ Child in my arms. The awe, the beauty, the unutterable joy and peace enfolding the babe is quite beyond expression and description. As I sat there with the babe a soft light shone and divine Mother appeared. Slowly I walked up and gave her the babe.

I would interpret this as a minor initiation of the soul into the consciousness in its own heart of the Christ Child. The giving back to the divine Mother of the child symbolises surrender of all that the soul most prized.

V

THE LOTUS POOL AND THE ELDER BRETHREN

White Eagle has taught us, when we have entered the infinite and eternal garden, to seek the inner secret garden where we will find a small, still pool on which float pure white lilies or lotus flowers.

First, consider the symbolism of still water. Water represents the emotional body and the psyche or soul; water is also a reflector and it is a purifier, therefore the still water of the lily pool symbolises a pure soul and stilled emotions —a clear reflector. To receive clear and perfect reception from above you must cultivate stillness and purity in the soul. If the water is ruffled the reflected image will be distorted.

Often I am asked, Why the lotus? What is its special significance? The lotus is an ancient and universal symbol held in veneration by inner brotherhoods of all time, and especially by the American Indians of the far past, the Maya race, the Egyptians, the Greeks, and of course in India and the Far East. It was a symbol closely connected with the lost continent of Mu, known to ancient peoples as the motherland, the cradle of the human race; which perhaps is one reason why meditation on this pure and exquisite flower can raise the consciousness right into the very heart and beginning of creation, the pulsating heart of love, the in-breathing and out-breathing of 'the breath of God.'

As the lotus spoke to these ancient peoples of the beginning of life on earth, so also it symbolised for them the birth and unfoldment of man's spiritual and soul powers. As explained in my first book, the development of psychic and spiritual powers takes place through the psychic centres, or as the eastern religions call them, the chakras. These are vortices of power in the etheric or soul body which occur at the centres corresponding to the main nerve ganglia in the physical body—the crown of the head, the brow, the throat, the heart, the spleen, solar plexus and the base of the spine— the root base, as it is sometimes referred to, or kundalini. Seen clairvoyantly these centres of power in the soul body look like lotus flowers, the number of petals varying according to the particular centre involved. For instance, the lower centres, or chakras, will have few petals but the heart has many, and the head centre, when fully developed, is described as the thousand petalled lotus.

When the aspirant starts to unfold his inner power, these centres quicken and develop and become exceedingly sensitive to impressions from the spirit spheres of life. As development proceeds, these 'lotus flowers' start to move in circular motion until they become pulsating vortices of light, made up of all the colours of the spectrum—a most beautiful sight for the clairvoyant. Through the practice of meditation and the manifestation of the Christ Spirit in life, these centres or chakras are stimulated to activity, and the solar body, or body of light, is developed, through which man receives all the spiritual sustenance he needs while on earth.

We can now understand why the lotus flower was held in such veneration by the inner brotherhoods of the past, and why the lotus flower is to be found on the carved stone work of many of their ancient temples.

We have seen that the lotus flower was the symbol of the ancient continent of Mu, the motherland of the human race. The lotus is therefore a symbol of divine love, which is the beginning of life, and the power which rules the universe. Where earthly love exists we see the reflection of the divine. In meditating on the sacred lotus flower with its petals opened to the sun, and the sunlight pouring from above into its golden heart, we find entry into the source of all creation, and to the heart of the heavenly mysteries.

At this point there comes the realisation of at-one-ment with the cosmic life, the ecstasy of becoming part of the whole of creation, the supreme joy of divine love.

It is in the realisation of this infinite and eternal love which encompasses all creation that the highest peak in meditation is reached—a never to be forgotten awareness of God in man and God within the lotus flower of the heart—the jewel (pure spirit) in the heart of the lotus.

This love becomes personified for me in the form of Jesus the Christ, man made perfect, the Christ man. From the beam of heavenly light which shines from the heavens into the centre of the lotus I have seen the perfect human form of the Christ gradually rise, sweet, pure and gentle, and clothed in white robes of dazzling sunshine. . . .

The Elder Brethren

Gradually, while we are meditating at the lotus pool, we become aware of the elder brethren who meditate with us. It is difficult, almost impossible, to separate the masters of the Great White Lodge one from the other and to know them as personalities, because a personality can only express one aspect of the whole being. So many names and initials are used to identify individual masters, but I think it is a mistake to limit the greatness of any of these great beings by labelling them. Moreover, at a certain level of spiritual development they are of one mind, they think and speak as one. Truly to make contact with a master soul the aspirant must rise to a very high spiritual level of consciousness, almost to cosmic consciousness, for on the lower planes he will meet with confusion. Sometimes the very confusion in which he finds himself is their way of testing his powers of discernment and discrimination. We have many lessons to learn before we shall be ready to see clearly and comprehend the truth about the masters. We can only strive to perfect our natures until we are worthy to be given more knowledge about them.

White Eagle says: 'Many times some of you have been so close to seeing the masters, and yet at the very last moment you have failed. The self has stood in the way. But when you begin to realise a little of the great love and tenderness which is watching every step of your development, every thought, every deed, it will perhaps encourage you to pick yourself up and start again with greater perseverance, in the sure knowledge that as soon as you are ready the master will manifest to you. He will not withhold his presence or his appearance from you when once you have earned the right to see him. It is only when you can recognise the qualities in a master that you will know him when he appears to you.

'The elder brethren are closely associated with you and with all souls of men and women who are on the path of light. It is a mistake to think that they are so exalted that they cannot, that they will not come to humble and simple people. Therefore do not think yourself beneath their notice. Remember that it is the truth in your heart, the sincerity of your aspirations which will bring these elder brethren to your side. We are told that the Master Jesus descended from the right hand of his Father to incarnate upon earth, to make himself one with simple folk. He went to all kinds of people, to the rich in spirit and to the poor in spirit. He was at-one with *all* men.

'So it is with the other great masters and saints of the past, some of whom you know by name and many more that you do not know. They can all come to you. They are at-one with your spirit, and the only dividing factor is your own unawakened state. Whenever you aspire in true love and worship of God, you are raised above all material conditions and you reach the level of consciousness where all are one in God. At that level the true communion of saints takes place.

'The elder brethren, as you are wont to call them, are all love, that is the keynote. When, through self-discipline, you are able to come into closer contact with them in meditation, if only for a flash, you will be overwhelmed with the feeling of love. Just to touch their aura will bring a sense of perfect harmony and love. Words cannot describe the state of mind and soul which comes to man through this communion with the wise ones; the intermingling of their natures, their aura with your own, blesses you with a heavenly state of consciousness, if only for a flash. When you come back to consciousness of the earth after such a meditation, you are dumb; no words can really describe what you feel and have seen, nor yet the effect such a vision has produced.' Here are some of my students' experiences:

▓ After the sounding of the AUM, I rose to the still pool and a group of white-robed elder brethren were waiting there and we all sat down cross-legged to contemplate the pure white lotus. I found that my own guide was seated next to me and I felt enfolded in his love and upheld by the strength of his spirit. I felt he helped me to concentrate upon the shining centre of the lotus, and as I did so, my emotions became stilled and all troubles fell away. I also became aware of the companionship of some of the other elder brethren in our group round the pool, and I felt such love and comradeship from them all. Then as I gazed at the lotus, I felt my guide lead me into its very heart and we were both kneeling before a golden altar in a golden temple, and received communion from the Christ himself.

You will notice the description of the perfect flower as floating on the *stilled* water, indicating the control of the emotional nature. In his book THE PATH OF THE SOUL, White Eagle speaks of this control of the emotions which comes with the water initiation. When the emotions are stilled and under the full control of the spirit, then the Christ Sun can shine forth from the soul in all its glory.

▓ I saw a golden triangle crowning the mountain peaks. On its topmost point was a pair of white wings and, reaching upwards, I found myself being carried on these wings

to the lotus pool. The pool was set in a circle
of golden light. I sat cross-legged beside it,
gazing into the still blue waters with the
lotus flower floating upon them, the jewel at
its centre. Gradually everything faded from
my vision except the jewel. Right in its heart
burned the white fire and from this white fire
there flowed through every facet of the jewel
rays of light of countless different colours.
The effect was glorious. This was the very
heart of the Christ, the white fire spreading
out in a divine harmony of colour to embrace
all creation. This was what our own hearts
must become, a replica of and at the same
time one with the heart of the Christ. As I
watched this jewel of infinite beauty, I became conscious of heavenly music.

I was alone, kneeling by the edge of the
pool, the palms of my hands flat on the stone
so that I could lean over. The lotus had sunk
to the bottom and was a tiny point of light
far away. As I gazed, the light drew nearer
and I saw in it the Christ Child lying on a bed
of rushes. I noticed how warm and pink the
flesh was and how a soft pink glow came from
his little body. The glow changed to gold and
then pure white and in place of the babe was
the jewel. It glowed and scintillated and then
such brilliance came from it I could not look.
It enveloped me. It enveloped the world and
it blessed and healed as the men and women
of earth looked up in longing and hope.

This suggests someone who has still a certain clinging to the mind of earth and the intellect, yet has just been touched by the light of the spirit; and during the meditation the jewel within the heart, the innermost light of the Christ Spirit (symbolised by the tiny babe) is just beginning to make its presence felt, and gradually it expands from the heart out into the whole of creation.

I tried to visualise the lotus with the jewel in its centre, and suddenly I seemed to be looking down on the most beautiful temple which was built in a complete circle, and seemed to be of a shining pale gold. In the centre of this temple was a most glorious still pool, very large and at one corner some white lilies floating. I sensed, rather than saw, a great host of people all sitting and lying round this pool, receiving healing, and as I gazed across from the other side of the pool, the figure of the Lord Jesus in a beautiful glistening white gown, slowly walked on to the water of the pool and stood in the centre, gazing with infinite love. Then he raised his eyes, and faded into the most beautiful fountain, containing all the colours of the rainbow, but which only replenished the pool without disturbing it. I could hear a voice saying, 'I am the living water' and then the fountain seemed to go higher and higher into the heavens, until I was in a beautiful lotus shaped temple, which had the petals curved downwards to form a circular floor; the outline of the petals was in a pale mauve and the centres of a white glowing light. I was told this was a temple of healing, and as we sent out the Light to humanity it radiated down to earth, and the whole earth was covered in blue flowers of every description, bluebells, violets, forget-me-nots and irises, all folding the earth in the mantle of blue.

The main feature of this symbol of the lily or lotus pool is its peace, stillness and absolute purity. One really becomes conscious of the union or at-one-ment of one's own being with the Christ. Purity, holiness, wholeness and perfection of life is felt by the soul who makes the true contact in meditation at the lily pool. It is truly a healing pool, the heart of the heavenly garden, or the heart of creation. It is the centre in man's consciousness from which spiritual life begins.

While meditating upon the jewel in the centre of the lotus a wonderful contact can be made with the Christ, the Son of God, and the realisation comes that the Christ is within one's own heart and that this light, this love can be used to illumine one's own life and give unlimited service to humanity. The following meditation examples will probably better help you to understand this than many pages of explanation would:

I was led to the lotus pool and found I had to plunge deep down into the water, and within these deepest waters of the pool was the lotus bearing within its cup the six-pointed star. The star sent out a shining radiance like a white flame, a bright movement of light. Within the star was the diamond, pure and untouchable, a still point of white light. This was the treasure to be found, the inmost secret. Then for a moment the diamond became a child within the star. At the same time, the star enclosing the diamond was in the heart of each one of us and everyone could use this star in the heart to send out the light and healing to those who were suffering in the world.

I was by a small pool with one violet lily in the centre, full of light. As I watched it, it closed up, and all around the light dimmed, and I realised it was symbolic of my earthly self. Quite suddenly it expanded again and I was in its centre. I realised I was praying, 'Breathe on me, breath of God, blend all my soul with thine, until this earthly part of me glows with thy fire divine.' As I said this it seemed as if I was enveloped in flames, deep blue outside and gold in the centre. I could feel the heat and the movement of this fire and yet I was not burned, and a voice said, 'These flames will absorb what is dross leaving only the gold.' I felt life-force pulsating all through my being (my physical body as well) and then it seemed as if a lid or small door was being opened on top of my head. Light seemed to stream from my whole being and I was able to direct it to various people I knew personally to be in need of help and healing, and to the whole world.

As we sat silently by the lily pool, the water became golden as though bathed in golden sunlight. We seemed somehow to be drawn right into the water and I could feel the easy movement of walking submerged in the golden liquid. Then suddenly I found myself gazing into the heart of a very pale rose— I can't describe how, but I seemed to be standing in the heart of this rose which expanded and expanded—the golden heart became a golden floor, the stamens stretched horizontally across the floor, making, as it were, golden paths from the centre. These then became vertical making the pillars of the temple—a temple open to the sky. Then the pale creamy walls, the petals of the rose, closed together again forming an almost gothic ceiling to the temple. It is difficult to describe how all this seemed to happen. Then from the golden centre of the rose, there came a huge golden altar, like a jewel with many facets.

Then I was aware of white-robed figures walking slowly in a circle around this altar. Then another circle appeared, and yet another, until the whole circular temple was full of white-robed figures moving in circles around the altar. After some time each of these circles moved out of the temple on one of the golden paths formed by the stamens of the rose, until only myself and my companions were left. A radiant being appeared in the front of the altar and, not by command, turned us outward and we were all directed to send a beam of light into the world, from our hearts.

VI

THE TEMPLE OF COMMUNION

When you have contacted your own guide or teacher by the lotus pool in the infinite and eternal garden, you may find that he leads you out of the garden to a heavenly temple. In this temple you may experience true spiritual communion. The following meditations are examples of this:

It was as if I was led by my guide to a temple, and all was so still and quiet. I have never been into one like this as it was illumined with the softest blue and silvery light. I could not see the form in the centre, but was deeply aware of it, and the perfect peace and all that pertained to the divine Mother. Gradually the silvery light became more golden, sun-lit and warm; and gradually there appeared the form of the Christ, the Golden One. What blessing! What a benediction! Then I saw the golden altar with the golden platter, and the bread and the golden cup of wine. I came to when I heard you describing the communion. My heart is full.

I walked into a garden filled with white

flowers of every description, lilies, white roses and white blossom. Ahead lay a calm blue lake with many lotus flowers. As I approached, a shaft of light made a path across the water. I was aware of a companion by my side in a white robe. He gave me a lighted candle and a single white rose. I followed him along the shaft of light walking on the calm water to the other side, and saw before me a round white shimmering temple, with steps leading up to it. Over the door was emblazoned a white rose in the heart of the cross within the circle of light. Inside the light intensified. Over the altar was the same emblem of the rose and the Lord Christ stood before it in a pure white robe with a gold and white rose on his breast. The petals unfurled. He came towards me and took from me the lighted candle and the white rose and it seemed as if both passed into my heart. I stayed worshipping. Presently I was aware that all our group were there and on the breast of each was this wonderful white rose.

I think that the lighted candle in this context signifies dawning spiritual knowledge. The white rose, pure divine love; it is a symbol of the age of brotherhood of the spirit.

I then aspired to the temple of brotherhood, which I knew was at the summit of the mountain. It was shrouded in mist and I had to wait until I had risen to a plane where it became 'concrete' and golden. I gave the password—LOVE—and was immediately inside the golden warmth of the temple. I saw the Plumed Serpents standing with their backs to the central altar and giving forth love. I knew I was not yet ready and knelt praying towards the central altar. I was taken down to a lower temple or crypt beneath this and laid upon a healing couch, which gradually passed under the central pillar of light from the temple above, until my heart was directly underneath. I was completely revitalised and joined the brethren; I was clothed in the raiment of a knight of the Star—silver, shining and pure—and I stood giving forth love with the rest.

The temple was of purest white and the light on the altar came from a golden lamp. I looked up to the roof where the huge blazing star seemed suspended or to float. The roof was made of the same semi-solid substance as the walls, with spaces in between open to the sky. Then I saw a lighthouse lamp in the centre of the star, revolving, sending its beams through the open spaces of the roof. Light was sweeping in great beams across the earth.

This temple on the hill gave me a wonderful feeling of service and watchful prayer, giving security and peace.

I suggest this was the Lodge above our own earthly temple where our own earthly brethren work on the inner planes for the upliftment of the world.

▓ Oh the freedom, the peace, as I sat in the temple of living light! I saw many symbols. It was so strange, I was seated in this temple and yet I saw another part of me, standing in the middle of a golden bridge and looking down into a deep chasm with a river flowing and so full of rocks and trees . . . all forms of life were there, but this time I felt no dread or fear of crossing the chasm, as I have before. Afterwards I felt such peace and at-one-ment as I stood in front of the altar. It seemed as if I was being blessed; the crown of my head, my heart, my throat, were being anointed with oil. I shall never forget this. Even the palms of my hands were anointed with oil, and a ring was placed on my finger.

Being anointed with oil suggests to me the gift of spiritual wisdom.

▓ After the sounding of the AUM I was standing in the temple of the white brethren —the temple with the great golden dome of light and the white iridescent pillars. The golden light from above seemed to pierce my head and I felt I was wearing a head-dress of light. A voice within was telling me to surrender my whole being to the golden light.

All was golden light—I know no words to express the feeling of wondrous joy and freedom. My heart was aflame and in my hands I held a crystal—the flame that was me came from the crystal, yet the flame too was a part of the white light—I was in it and of it.

I was moved through a curtain of falling water. The flame was not dimmed by the water but rather the drops of water around me became more sparkling. I was by a great pillar of light, from the top of this pillar swayed great plumes of light—I passed into this light, I was of this pillar of light. I was at the centre of the universe and I, like every man, had been here, a part of it, since the beginning of time.

Water is symbolic of the psyche or soul. The drops of water which became more sparkling indicate that the soul becomes more beautiful and more shining by the increasing strength and power of the divine spirit, or the Christ Light within the heart. A glimpse or flash of cosmic consciousness.

I close this chapter with White Eagle's own words, in which he takes us into the Temple of the Brotherhood, where we commune with the Golden One:

'We take you in spirit to the Temple of the Brotherhood. You think of the spirit world as being above you, naturally, because you think of spiritual things as being in heaven and you are accustomed to think of heaven as up above you. But spirit life is not necessarily away in space. When we take you to the temple of the Brotherhood we say, "Come, we will raise you to the Lodge above," but you do not move. You remain sitting where you are; yet something happens to your mind and brain. You are conscious of harmony and beauty; and all earthly material objects fade right away from you. As you concentrate on the temple of the Brotherhood, you are in it. The object of the Brotherhood's work is to unite the spiritual and physical life in the soul of man.

'In order to help you to understand the unity of life we try to help you to turn inward, to find the entrance to heaven through your own spirit, your own heart, for you will only find entrance to the heaven world through your heart chakra, or rather, through the point of union between the heart and the higher mind, between the heart chakra and the head chakra. When this union between heart and head has come about you will have learnt the secret of reaching the heaven world. The heaven world is neither "here" nor "there"; it is everywhere, it is within yourself.

'Now let us sit quietly, use your spiritual vision, your imagination and gradually you will become aware that you are sitting in a golden temple, with tall fluted pillars supporting the fan-vaulting of the roof. Feel in your heart and spirit the gentle atmosphere of the Golden One. Feel his influence and the beauty around you . . .

'He stands before you . . .

'He is giving into your soul the golden message of resurrection. Very special Brothers of the Star are helping you to realise this message of the arisen Christ, the Christ which now at this moment is rising in *you*, cleansing, comforting, healing . . .

'Rays from his being penetrate and enfold you in the golden atmosphere of the Brotherhood temple.

'He who is enthroned in this golden place is like the ancient pictures of a sun sending out its rays. This sun is *here*, and your hearts are penetrated by the rays of the Christ Spirit or the petals of the golden flower.

'Build in your soul or in your vision the golden temple, built with the very soul substance of your own being, and of the collective Brotherhood who are united in their purpose of giving the golden light into the world and bringing upon earth the golden age, the kingdom of heaven.'

VII

THE VALUE OF MEDITATION
IN EVERYDAY LIFE

In this chapter we will touch on the value of meditation in everyday life. This may seem strange to some readers; but a mystic is not impractical. The power which comes to him as a result of his becoming one, through meditation, with universal Mind, with God, enables him to attend to earthly matters in greater detail, with greater courage, with quickened, wiser mind.

White Eagle says: 'In ages past the masters and God-men taught their pupils how to meditate and to build a bridge between themselves and the heaven world. They taught them how to live in accord with cosmic and natural law, so that even while still in a physical body they would realise themselves to be forever within the mind and heart of their Creator.

'To a much lesser degree the younger brothers now on earth are being taught the ways of harmony and health and happiness. But, brethren, we all have to learn the one simple and vital lesson—to love one another, to love life, to love all the produce of the earth, and to live and breathe and even die, when the time comes, within the consciousness of the everlasting and eternal spirit of love and peace.

'No man can serve two masters, and those who are on the path should give all their heart, their life, to God and their spiritual companions and guides. When you are troubled by the conflicts of earthly and ignorant minds, turn your thoughts immediately to the spiritual life and to the brethren who are there protecting you as you give yourselves into their keeping. Do not think about earthly conflicts because if you live in accord with divine law you are helping the world, you are helping all mankind as surely, indeed more surely, than if you were doing work of a material nature which would not be as effective.

'You all want to be practical and efficient. Well, start upon yourself, upon your life, by eating pure food, drinking pure water, breathing pure air; by thinking purely, by ordering your life harmoniously—leading a gentle, quiet life, controlling unruly emotions and thoughts. Meditate morning and night—first a morning prayer to your Creator that you may be His servant this day; and as you go to rest at night, a prayer that you may contact the highest in your sleep state. This is most important because when you go to sleep, you go out into the etheric and spirit world; and if instead of going to bed with your mind like a rag bag, cluttered with rubbish, you can go to sleep with a mind set upon God and a pure spiritual state of life, then rather than just hovering above your body as you sleep, or clinging to earthly conditions, you will go straight into elysian fields where you will be instructed by your teachers in the temple of knowledge and wisdom. When you return to your physical body in the morning you will feel so happy. You will say: "I have had a wonderful night and I feel so different." Of course; you have been in the world of light.

'So we suggest that you prepare yourselves the very last thing before falling asleep, even if it is only for two or three minutes. The angels, the messengers of God, will be waiting to guide you towards the temple of wisdom and if you go with them you will absorb into your higher mind wisdom which in time will percolate through into your brain. But you will have to discipline and train yourselves.

'We suggest that you begin your meditation just with thoughts of God, of His ineffable love, and of the spirit. Dwell often on these thoughts until the time comes when they govern your actions and reactions so that as the Christ Light within you grows stronger you spontaneously react in the Christ way to any challenge in your life.

'Do not think this impossible; it is the natural way for your spiritual growth, your spiritual life to express itself. First establish firmly in your consciousness that you are primarily spirit and not body. Act by the spirit, let goodness and love always be your guide, no matter what your circumstances and conditions. You cannot go wrong if you follow the true inner light which is the voice of God, of the Christ.'

Through meditation, then, one finds the inner centre of peace, and the truth which brings answers to every problem of the earthly life. While the mind is busy going over and over a problem the answer completely eludes the physical brain. But in the quiet of meditation, when the mind is still, true help comes from the spirit guide and from the spirit, the voice of God within oneself. During meditation the higher mind is stimulated and used by the divine spirit to guide and help man for his own good as well as the good of the community.

Meditation is, of course, the finest source of help in solving day to day problems, and in bringing spiritual insight and understanding of the wider issues of life. Sometimes a student cannot with his earthly mind comprehend some aspect of ancient wisdom (for example, the truth of reincarnation, or the relationship of Jesus and the Christ, two common stumbling blocks). No amount of mental study makes any difference, in fact often greater confusion and uncertainty result. However, in a state of true meditation a new understanding can be born; an understanding of the heart, which no mental argument can ever again shake.

An important point to remember when seeking the answer to an earthly problem in the deep stillness of true meditation is that the problem must quite deliberately be put out of mind. True contact with those spheres from which help comes cannot be made while the mind struggles with earthly conditions. Just as the physical body must be completely comfortable and at ease, so too must the lower mental and emotional bodies. Of course I know that this is very much more easily said than done, and when one is in the midst of a problem it is very difficult not to keep thinking about it. Nevertheless a conscious effort must be made to put this on one side and to concentrate on the divine spirit and heavenly life.

The first of the following meditations exemplifies my point about endeavouring to free oneself from an earthly trouble so that spiritual help can come:

I had a difficult time during the meditation, but it was very good for me. I could get nowhere at all at first, in fact I felt bound down, chained. I work with a man who can be rather unpleasant occasionally, and this had been the case recently. I thought it might affect my meditation and it did. I tried everything I could think of to break the bonds, but got nowhere until I thought of the cross of matter with the rose at the centre and then I found I was on the cross, lying bound. After a time I heard a voice say that what was binding me down was not what this man had said to me but my lack of forgiveness. I had been talking forgiveness but not feeling it deep inside.

This meditation exemplifies the truth of White Eagle's words, that it is not what happens to us that matters so much as our own reactions that cause us to be unhappy.

※ I heard the words, 'Be confident.' This proved to be the most helpful thing possible, since, throughout the following meditation, whenever I 'woffled' I just said, 'Be confident' and went right there again. It was most encouraging how these two words lifted me up to where I had been before I distracted myself. In previous meditations I found it difficult to return, once having 'woffled.'

This illustrates the unwanted intrusion of the lower earthly mind and the power which is in the divine will within the pupil. Meditation is an exercise of the divine will deep within the soul of the meditator.

The following is a clear example of comfort received in meditation after an earthly upset.

※ When I found the lotus pool I was overwhelmed with its stillness. The birds stopped singing and there was no sound, and then I felt infinite purity. Then I was conscious of a still white figure standing on the bank, and somehow I knew it was the Master Jesus. I went to him and knelt at his feet and was comforted. His feet were so beautiful and I kissed them. Then, foolishly, I thought of having failed my driving test and I seemed to hear His voice, 'Don't worry, my child, this is only an earthly thing,' and I felt his strength and his holiness pouring into me. So I rose with confidence and went out from him into the world of spirit.

At the lotus pool there is always this sense of deep peace, purity and holiness or wholeness.

There were times during the meditation when I lost the picture (but never the contact in the heart) and at one of these times I found myself shaping a clay bowl. This kept appearing afterwards and later on I gave it or held it up to somebody, saying that there were flowers in it. Somebody tapped it saying, 'It rings true' and it was for me for the rest of the meditation. I had a feeling that it would be filled, but this didn't happen. I suppose the bowl is myself, and I wonder if anyone really did say, 'It rings true' or whether this was wishful thinking. (I'm too well aware of the flaws.)

This meditation signifies aspiration and a desire to be true and to always ring true. This is one of the first essentials of brotherhood.

I believe that in some ashrams in the east the students learn spiritual truth through creative work—some craft, like pottery. The Christ Spirit is the potter, the clay is the soul, the potter's wheel is human experience or the wheel of life.

Sometimes an impression is given but the student is left to find the answer:

※ I felt once again a strong grip on my right shoulder during this meditation. I wondered if someone was trying to make me do something, or stop me from doing something. Can you tell me?

This is an example of the development of the sense of feeling. An impression such as this student describes means that someone in spirit was giving strength, understanding and encouragement to the pupil.

※ I experienced a useful and practical meditation in which I held in the light many earthly conditions connected with my work, and I felt I was learning the lesson of being less driven and anxious but rather working quietly from the centre of love and positive thought deep within my own being.

This is an excellent interpretation of a spiritual message, which is teaching the student a profound truth. Let us put it in another way and say, the student was being taught how to 'rest in the Lord,' and to control the emotional body by bringing troubles to the great solver of all problems, God. If you turn your mind away from earthly troubles and centre your thoughts upon God (light) instead of on troubles (darkness) the darkness is swallowed up in the light.

✻ The main lesson I am learning at present in my meditations is not to feel so inadequate and driven as I have hitherto. The outer self and appearances do not matter as much as I thought. More has been achieved from within than I realised; life is less intense and terrifyingly insecure; I am no longer alone.

This shows a big step forward on the path. It is not always in seeing pictures or hearing the voices of spirit companions that progress is made, but in the gradual unfoldment of the wisdom within your own spirit.

✻ I felt rather than saw, I felt the very tired part of me was taken away to rest, and I felt so wonderfully soothed and at such peace, and then could enjoy the beautiful garden and the golden light all round me. I went into the healing temple and saw Jesus with his healing angels; I saw the beautiful pillars of light and the patients being healed by coloured rays. I came back to earth feeling so refreshed and full of wonder.

The meditator went in full consciousness to the temple of healing, and undoubtedly received healing, both for soul and body.

✻ I had been concerned before the meditation about the state of world affairs—there seemed to be fighting almost everywhere, but I managed to put this out of my mind

68

and made a good contact in the heavenly
garden; then I was thrilled to see streams
of light like searchlights being directed all
over the earth for the healing, illumination
and the blessing of all mankind and pene-
trating into the dark astral regions for the
healing of our brethren there. On returning
to the earthplane I felt that all was well and
that the light within seemed to shine all the
time.

This is a splendid illustration of the activity
of the White Brotherhood on the inner planes
of life, where they are working continuously for
the healing of men and nations and to help
those in bondage on the dark astral planes beyond death.

Proof of the efficacy of this work was given to
me when a woman asked for help for her dying
brother, whose life had been such that she
feared he might find himself in darkness. She
hoped that the spiritual healing would help him
when he awakened on the other side of life, and
some time later he returned to his sister through
another medium. He said he had been be-
wildered and lost when he first passed on. Then
a great beam of light like a searchlight enfolded
him, picked him up and carried him out of the
darkness into a lovely place in the spirit world.

As one who has to learn through succes-
sive realisations rather than by visions or
symbols which rarely come my way, it is not

easy to put into words what I have learnt during meditation. I think the overall gain has been the realisation of the solid reality of the higher worlds compared to the misty fluctuations of the physical life. Perhaps I could say a realisation of love itself as a living being, without human shape but to whom the phrase 'holding out its arms' can give a symbolic expression. I believed this before but had not experienced it, just as one may believe in some far country, and then get the opportunity to visit it and turn the belief into knowledge.

When, during the meditation we finally arrived at the temple, and through the help of the great masters in meditation round the oblong table, we were raised sufficiently to be able to enter and look on the great central flame, the realisation came as never before that a 'heart beats there' within whose conscious love and understanding all human sorrows and anxieties are dissolved. The direction to walk into that light was obeyed in visualisation and though that might appear to be an immolation it is to be immediately absorbed into peace and love beyond the human comprehension. The words 'Thine is the kingdom, the power and the glory' can be understood anew and the great heart of the Father says, 'What is mine is thine' and in that at-one-ment I realised I am that Light as are all men and all beings whatsoever.

This meditation is an excellent example of the arisen Christ in man, when he is able to state categorically, 'Now I know.' It illustrates the difference between knowledge coming through books or reading the opinions of others, and the wisdom and knowledge which is attained through the awakening of the Christ Spirit in man. It shows the difference between mind and intellect and an inward becoming or birth of the Christ Spirit.

In the garden of remembrance I returned to the pool and gazed again at the reflection of the Star. While there I had an experience I find hard to describe. The reflection was the expression of the aphorism, 'As above, so below.' With that came the realisation that all is well—the plan is perfect and nothing can destroy it. With this realisation love, joy and peace swept through my being in waves of bliss. All those in the temple said amen, and we said amen. Afterwards White Eagle stood with his back to the altar and smiled on us.

One has to remember the statement, 'As above, so below.' In meditation we are the receivers of the light. If we realise that the human soul is the reflector of the spiritual life, we can understand the importance of practising the art of achieving stillness in the soul.

So many are eager to give help in this

troubled world and often meditation can show the way:

I was alone but so peaceful and walked along a wide path and saw ahead a great shining almost transparent white star. A tall white figure stood in the centre and beckoned me to come, as I hesitated. In the heart all was light and I, too, became filled. The Star magnified until it encompassed all and I was aware of many people all clad in white with a silver cross on their breasts and before them a figure on a white horse. Beyond them rose wide steps leading to a white temple, and on its pinnacle was a great star pulsating with all colours and rays. I entered the temple which was full of diffused light of many colours. Leading off were large rooms and entering I realised that rays were being directed to trouble spots on earth and many brothers were there ready to be sent anywhere to help. I felt a burning desire to help and yet somehow knew I must grow strong within myself, but that if I were patient I would be used, for all that is good in one is of God, and the rest, God willing, will fall away. That which is good is never wasted and can always be used in service to help those in need.

VIII

THE USE OF THE FIVE SENSES IN MEDITATION

In training ourselves to become receptive to the impressions from the spirit world which is all around us it is important to remember that every one of our senses has its spiritual counterpart. We are wonderfully made by our Creator with powers which enable us to respond as clearly to the influence and impressions of the higher levels of life as to those of the physical level.

In White Eagle's own words: 'We continually remind you that the spiritual world and the physical world are closely inter-related. Indeed, this interpenetration and interrelation of all life is one of the first lessons to be learnt on the spiritual path. There is no separation between the spiritual realms of life and the physical, between God and man. Man is the microcosm, and contains within his physical, etheric, mental and spiritual bodies exactly the same life principles as are contained in the macrocosm. Hence the saying written over the entrance to ancient mystery schools: "Man, know thyself, and thou shalt know God and the universe."

'Man's five senses enable him to be aware of

life on the physical plane; they do not function only through the physical body, however, but also through the higher vehicles, the spiritual bodies of man. Each sense has its counterpart in the subtler bodies of man. Something of the spiritual aspect of the senses will be understood if they can be related to the five elements— Earth, Air, Fire, Water and Ether.

'Let us first consider the sense of sight: Light reveals the physical world to us—fire gives us light. Therefore we relate the element Fire to the sense of sight. At the higher level, through the light of the spiritual sun, the Christ dwelling in the heart, the inner eyes can be opened so as to reveal the inner worlds and the light of God or Christ in your brother man.

'You must have the light in your own heart before you can see God, the Light, in others. When the inner sight is developed, you are able to see God in all creation. Your eyes being touched with the divine fire, you see beauty in all things.'

It is not difficult to become aware of the spiritual counterpart of the sense of sight. In most cases inner sight is the first sense to develop. The student of the art of meditation expects to see with his inner eyes but is often quite un-aware of the other senses which can and should be brought into use. Some students, on the other hand, find it very difficult to 'see' any-thing at all, and often feel they have completely failed as a result. If this is true in your case, do remember that meditation is not just seeing, it is hearing, smelling, tasting, touching and feeling. You may not see, but you may hear heavenly music or feel a deep sense of peace and at-one-ment with God. Gradually you will learn to develop and use the spiritual counterpart of all your senses.

'The sense of hearing we relate to the element Air, which carries sound waves to your ears. But if you will try to close your outer sense of hearing and listen deeply for the "sound within the silence" you will hear a sound which is not purely physical. As you learn to attune your hearing to these inner sound waves, reaching out and beyond the physical to the inner hearing, you will hear the great Word of power, the creative Word, pervading the air. Listen, for instance, when you are in the country . . . gradually you will begin to become aware of an underlying sound in all nature, the great AUM . . . the voice of cosmic being.'

This inner sense of hearing is beginning to develop in the two meditations quoted below:

> I heard a group of brethren singing a song or hymn, and the glory of it floated out through the arches of the temple down to the world below. The music floated out as tangible gossamer threads; I watched them and saw them fall as dew on weeds, and bring forth flowers; and I saw the people who heard the thread of that heavenly music rise up and aspire, though they did not know from whence the aspiration came.

 I seemed to be at one with all nature; I heard the plop of fish leaping out of the lake, and the gentle lap, lap of the water on the shore; I heard the humming of the bees and the flutter of passing butterflies; I heard the rustle of small animals in the nearby wood and felt an overwhelming communion and unity with all this life and indeed with all creation.

These are good examples of the beginning of clairaudience or clear hearing in the soul. All these sounds in nature make a lasting impression on the soul, remaining in the memory to be awakened and stimulated in meditation.

Clairaudience or clear hearing can come at different levels of consciousness. True clairaudience comes on the inner spiritual levels without any physical sound. Sometimes the voice comes from the inner world at the etheric level, when it is called the 'direct voice,' or 'direct hearing,' but this is not the way one hears in meditation. It is an inner voice, the voice in the silence, that is heard in deep meditation, which is not the same as a semi-physical voice which comes through psychic materialisation of the dense etheric atoms.

White Eagle relates the sense of smell to the element Earth, and says that with this sense, the finer essences of life within the earth can be detected. He says: 'You can, if you will, smell the fragrance, the life, the very essence of the earth; and you can penetrate even beyond this to absorb or inhale the essence of the cosmic body. Do you see what this means? Through your physical sense of smell, you may penetrate into the life of God. All five senses, though, are fundamentally of the cosmic body.'

White Eagle continues: 'The inner sense of smell can bring an exquisite experience to the soul. Sometimes the masters will fill a room with the scent of a particular flower; and discarnate souls can often use this means to assure their loved ones left on earth that they are not far away, but close by.'

The sense of smell seems to be almost easier for the beginner at meditation to develop than that of hearing. Many of my students have mentioned smelling the clear fresh water while seated at the lily pool, the perfume of the flowers in the garden of reunion, or the perfume they associate with a particular loved one or elder brother. Many of you will know how often White Eagle guides his pupils to inhale the fragrance of the rose. I have one example I should like to quote here:

I felt a pervading holiness and purity in the temple. There was a central altar upon which was placed a perfect rose. The elder brethren formed a ring around this altar and I joined them and we all inhaled the perfume of the rose. The perfume seemed to be the essence of peace and tranquillity which we inhaled and absorbed into ourselves. Gradually the rose took the form of a grail cup, and seemed to come to each one of us in turn to sip the wine—which never got any less because it seemed to be invisibly and perpetually replenished from the bottom. I knew that this was the wine which feeds, sustains, and maintains us. I felt so strongly the nutriment of the wine and the effect of the perfume.

This meditation clearly illustrates the use of perfume as a means of aspiration and of making a stronger and clearer contact than might otherwise be possible.

The sense of taste is related by White Eagle to the element of Water, and he says: 'Drink the water from a running stream, drink the sparkle and sunshine that gives it life. Do you taste water only? No, there is more; an indefinable, indestructible component is there. You drink the very life-force of the earth. Through the sense of taste, which we relate to the Water element, you can create harmony and peace in the kingdom of yourself. On the other hand, you can create a tempest, create havoc, in the physical body. The sense of taste will create a peaceful and well-ordered microcosm or it will do the reverse.'

On one occasion during my own personal meditations I found myself walking through a garden towards my teacher's residence, and I was surprised to see fruit vines climbing up the supporting pillars inside the entrance hall. My companion, seeing my astonishment, said, 'Pick the fruit and taste it.' I did so, and I find it almost impossible to describe what it was like. It was a soft fruit with an exquisite flavour, which I felt was feeding and enriching my whole being. In other words it was the fruit of heaven. This little incident impressed me very deeply; it made me realise that all form in the spirit life is created from the substance of the cosmic body. It helped me to understand the brotherhood of life and that God, or spirit, interpenetrates every form of life.

White Eagle says, 'The sense of touch or "feeling" we relate to the etheric body, and to the element Ether. If the etheric body is driven out of the physical body, the physical body has no feeling; a fact demonstrated when a patient is given an anaesthetic, the effect of which is to drive out the etheric body. It is the etheric body (so closely related to the nervous system) which creates sensitivity to touch in the physical body.'

The higher counterpart of the sense of feeling or touch seems to develop quite easily for the student of meditation; indeed, as I explained at the beginning of the chapter, some students find they can 'feel' yet cannot 'see.' A common experience in meditation is to feel cool green grass underfoot as one walks in the infinite and eternal garden; to feel the rough bark of a tree, or to touch the surface of the water and find it cool and refreshing. I have known students feel the soft fur of animals, or hard roughness of stone.

One student writes:

❖ During the meditation I felt as though I was being anointed for I was aware of someone touching my forehead and drops of water seemed to rest there, but I could not see anything while I was experiencing this. I heard the words within myself, 'He anointeth thy head with oil—thy cup runneth over. . .'

In the following meditation the sense of touch and feeling is quite clearly developed:

❖ In meditating on the sun in the centre of the group, I became a part of it, as if it were a flying saucer and I was sitting on it. From outside this glowing circle I saw many, many buildings far below, some with lighted windows, others grey. I seemed to move through a sky for the panorama kept changing, but always of streets and buildings. Most of the lighted windows were in churches. My hands, grasping the edge of the sun disc, felt it firm to touch.

The next two examples are interesting as both demonstrate the feeling of the change in physical form which can take place during meditation:

❖ After climbing up the mountain, the golden path leading to the temple opened to receive me. I then felt very small, transparent, and white—reduced to practically nothing—and so was able to pass through the gates, even though they were closed, as a wraith passes through solid matter.

※ I looked at the diamond in the heart of the lotus and I thought that if I could shrink to the size of an atom I could enter the diamond which would not be exactly cosmic consciousness but perhaps a higher consciousness. Unfortunately I found I could not shrink enough for I had too many material thoughts and encumbrances surrounding me, but perhaps some day. . .!

In the next account, the student's sense of touch has been used to convey to his soul an awareness of communion, or union, with the Christ Spirit, or, in White Eagle's words 'to feel the form of the Lord.'

※ Then I was slowly but completely taken over from behind by a higher form of light. There was quite a long process of mingling the atoms of every organ of the two bodies. For the first time the words 'nearer than breathing, closer than hands or feet' made real sense to me. It was as if previously the atomic structure of my body was only half there, and needed this fulfilment, this union with the Christ Spirit, to complete my being. I was overwhelmed with a deep sense of peace, and longed to share with and send out to others some of this love which filled my heart.

Here are some closing words from White Eagle: 'Use your senses with reverence and with the highest endeavour, thus opening the gateways for help to flow to you from the invisible worlds. Remember the need for balance in your lives, and temperance. Never go to extremes: cultivate harmony and thus increase your awareness of God. You can taste God in the food you eat, in the water you drink; through your sense of smell you can inhale the essence of God; through your sight you can see light, which is God; through hearing you increase your awareness of beauty . . . God. This is the whole purpose of your life on earth—to increase your awareness of God.'

IX

COMMUNION WITH YOUR LOVED ONE IN SPIRIT

Many people write to me when sorrowful following the loss of a much loved companion, and White Eagle and I do our best to help them find comfort through knowledge of the reality of the life of the spirit, and to show them how a real communion with their loved one in spirit can take place; for it is this inner communion, spirit with spirit, which brings lasting proof of life beyond death—a proof which no intellectual argument or mental reasoning can shake. A message through a third party can indeed help, and White Eagle has helped many, and given very evidential messages, but in the main it is through a person's own endeavour to rise in consciousness and find communion with his or her loved one at a spiritual level that lasting proof and reunion is found.

When seeking to communicate with a loved one in spirit, remember that we on the physical plane have to do our part to help those in spirit by building what I can only describe as an etheric bridge between their state of life and ours. Here I must explain that we can only contact the differing spheres of life—the physical, mental, emotional, and spiritual—by utilising the substance of that particular sphere. For instance, during this physical life we communicate with one another through use of our physical senses. Therefore, when a discarnate soul wishes to make a physical contact with someone on earth, he or she has to draw upon physical substance taken from the body of a medium or from the sitters in the group in order to make this contact or give the evidence. This will produce a physical manifestation such as a touch, a sound, or even a materialised form. While this form of communication at a physical level has been scientifically proven and many books have been written on the subject by people who have received proof of life after death in this way, man is now evolving beyond the need for such physical manifestations. We move forward to a more spiritual communion with those who live in the spirit spheres.

White Eagle therefore teaches his students that they should endeavour to raise their consciousness to the spiritual level instead of trying to pull the loved one down to their own level. The way to do this, he says, is through meditation; and the key to meditation, as I have already explained, is use of one's highest imagination—of the creative power which God has implanted in every soul.

Imagination is vital for spiritual perception, the very key of the door leading into the higher and subtler spheres, and those wishing to develop clear vision and commune with loved ones in spirit through meditation must work to develop their highest, purest and most God-like imagination. This is a subtle thing to understand, and only practice will bring conviction that, through his imagination and meditation, the aspirant is being helped and guided by higher intelligences who have him in their charge.

As we have already found, each of the five senses has its etheric counterpart, the sensitivity of which can be developed through exercising the gift of imagination. I discovered this myself many years ago when giving public demonstrations. For instance, the sense of smell—smells such as those of hay, of certain flowers, of newly dug earth, and so on—was often used to convey the identity of the communicator. As an example, an ardent gardener was identified by the smell of newly dug earth. On another occasion a widow came to me for consolation. Although she was not wearing perfume or flowers, as she approached a strong scent of violets wafted towards me and filled the room. Then, as I went into meditation, I saw a large bowl of freshly picked, dew-drenched violets placed before her. If only she could have seen or smelt them, how lovely it would have been for her! When I told her what I was seeing, she exclaimed, 'Oh! It is my darling husband, I know it is, because this was our favourite flower. Whenever an anniversary occurred, he always bought me a bouquet of violets.'

Once, when I was meditating with a pupil,

I heard strains of music, a piece which turned out to be a favourite of both the communicating spirit and the sitter. A very simple proof, but deeply significant to the sitter.

When seeking contact with your loved one in spirit, do not think of him or her as having gone far from you, and thus surround yourself with a barrier of doubt and grief. He or she is very close to you in spirit and only the barrier of your sorrow prevents your reunion. Remember that where there is true love there can never be separation of the spirit, but you yourself have to make the effort to rise above earthly conditions to meet your loved one in the spirit body. To do this, first lay aside all the cares of the physical life, all sadness, and try to imagine the glorious soul world in which your loved one is now living.

In every meditation class I lead my students to the place which White Eagle calls the garden of reunion, where they meet and commune with those they love. If you are seeking such communion, start your meditation in the usual way by endeavouring to reach the highest peak of the golden mountain, rise in consciousness into that golden light . . . and then try to create a beautiful garden, the garden of reunion and walk in this garden in imagination. You will find there is an inner rose garden full of scented blooms. Try to inhale their exquisite perfume and feel the peace of heaven fill your being. In this garden you will see a white seat; sit down on this seat and mentally talk to your loved one.

He or she may come to you almost immediately and you will be able to speak together and find joy in one another's companionship. If you commune in spirit and mentally speak to your loved ones, they will hear your thoughts and understand what you are saying to them, and you will either imagine that you hear their voice, or the words they are saying will come into your mind and you will know the message as surely as if you heard the physical voice.

You may think on reading this that it would all be imagination but, as I have explained, imagination is the key into the soul world. Remember that the substance used to create forms on the earth plane is physical. And when we are working on the etheric or soul plane the substance is etheric or soul substance. So your creative imagination, the picture you create in your higher mind out of soul substance, is as solid and real to the people living on that plane as physical form is to those on earth. By using your imagination you are unlocking the door which separates you and you are giving your loved one the opportunity to contact you, free from the cloud of sorrow, in the age-old garden of reunion.

White Eagle says: 'In order to receive impressions from the inner or soul world, it is of the utmost importance that the activity of the brain should be stilled. You cannot receive impressions from the soul world if the brain is too active. We take an illustration for you of a pool of clear water. If the water is ruffled then the impressions made upon that water become distorted, but if that pool is absolutely still it can reflect perfectly. We use this illustration because water is associated with the soul, with the psyche. If the soul or the emotions of the instrument are disturbed, the impressions from the soul world become distorted and in this way misleading communications can be received from our world of spirit; but when you can withdraw from the turmoil of worldly thought and disturbed emotion into a state of peace and tranquillity, slowly you become attuned to the soul world and can receive clear impressions from it.

'When you are thinking of those whom you love most who are in the world of spirit, try to realise that there is no difference between here and where they are. They are with you. They may not be with you in a physical body but they are with you in a soul body or a body of finer ether, and in your mind, in the spiritual consciousness, there is no separation at all. When death takes place it is like slipping off an old coat and the one who slips it off is exactly the same as before except that he or she knows freedom and lightness and greater comfort. But as far as communion, communication with loved ones goes, there need be no break—life just goes on. We do want to help you all to understand that life is eternal.

'Life, whether at a physical level or at a soul level, is still *life*. The habitual thought of the individual is externalised on the soul plane and when the mind has been trained to be direct and sound, then its communications will be clear and direct and sound. From this you will begin to understand the importance of the development of the power of thought, and that it should be developed on the right lines. It should be good thought, God thought; it should be beautiful thought. When thoughts are beautiful, the surroundings are beautiful, the externalisation of the soul is beautiful.

'If your heart is pure and you are aspiring to serve your fellows through your love for the Great White Spirit, you cannot be deceived in what you see and hear in the world of spirit. There is no separation between spirit life and the physical life except through man's own wilful denial of this ancient wisdom, this age-old truth.'

The following are descriptions of the garden of reunion as seen by my students:

I was taken to the most beautiful garden I have ever seen. I saw soft green lawns surrounded by fragrant flowering bushes; delightful rockeries with pretty little plants tumbling from every nook and cranny, and small rushing streams with pretty waterfalls; herbaceous borders in every colour on either side of paths which converged on a central sundial; and in the distance a parkland leading to a lake, and then the sea and mountain peaks beyond. But I was drawn from my wrapt contemplation of this scene to take a small paved path which led to what seemed the very heart of the garden—the inner rose garden. I opened the little wrought iron gate and came into my dream garden. The air was heavy with the perfume of countless roses and I followed one of the small paths between the beds and found myself in a secluded rose-bower. There I sat on the white seat and quietly absorbed the beauties all around. I saw my dear one come towards me with open arms and he enfolded me to his heart. I knew that here, in the inner rose garden—the garden of reunion—we were deeply united spirit to spirit in a pure love quite unclouded by any material care or earthly problem.

We were taken to the garden of reunion where we visited the cleansing pool, and I was very conscious of my father and mother (who passed on some time ago) and of my guide. They were all around me and beckoning me upward. There was a lot of laughter because I found the way so steep and was struggling, whereas my mother (who could never climb hills in her physical body) was able to run up quite easily. She seemed so young, just as I had known her long before her illness, and somehow illumined and radiant. I knew she was deeply happy in her new life, and to be reunited once more with her dear husband. After this experience I could never doubt the truth of the beautiful life which awaits us after death.

※ In that peaceful age-old garden I was reunited with my son. As we strolled arm in arm along the paths between the glorious roses, he told me of his new life in this beautiful world of spirit. I had thought his death so young such a waste, and many times asked, 'Why? Why?' But now I knew: he was continuing his studies, learning so much in the temples of wisdom that he could never have learnt on earth, and had much work before him. He was happier than I had ever known him.

※ We were called to the garden of reunion, and as usual I had difficulty because I wondered what this had to do with me as I did not know anyone who was dead. Then suddenly I realised for the first time that the garden of reunion was where one's special friends were, not just those who had died recently. Immediately I realised this I met my guide and friends I recognised from past incarnations and felt a really wonderful sense of waves and waves of throbbing love vibrating from each to each. I was so happy, it was such a wonderful reunion and I realised again our limited conception of time and space.

X

INSIGHT INTO PAST LIVES

A particularly fascinating aspect of meditation often develops as the student advances. Once one accepts the truth of reincarnation, it profoundly affects not only one's everyday thought and relationship with others but also one's whole approach to life's circumstances. This applies even more to the student who, accepting the truth of reincarnation, is learning the art of meditation.

In the raised consciousness of the meditative state a whole new world is revealed wherein the student may not only savour the beauties of the spirit life and learn of the heavenly mysteries from his guide, he may also be shown glimpses of past lives on earth. These glimpses into the akashic records are not shown to the student 'just for fun' but are used to give valuable guidance, and possibly insight into the reasons for certain conditions in his present life.

No limitation of space or time exists in this state of consciousness. Whilst one can be in London one minute, by the power of thought one can instantly in the next second be in Africa, Australia or America, or indeed anywhere else in this world or the next. The minds of people many miles apart can be trained to pick up messages from other human minds. Similarly, in the raised state of consciousness, one can tune into lives in different times and places, all within a few minutes of earthly time. As White Eagle says: 'We can relive the past by the same process which you are learning to use in your meditations. We can live at any time throughout the ages in any condition, any nation, any part of the earth and any part of the solar system. We can live in full consciousness in other places, in other worlds, in other spheres of life.'

Sometimes my students describe how they have been led by their guide into a temple of wisdom and have seen what they take to be incidents from past lives shown on a screen. Others find they walk straight into a past life; they feel as though they are living it again, and notice that they are dressed in the clothes of that time.

Many of my readers may already know my book THE ILLUMINED ONES in which I have described how I relived past lives in South America and in Egypt. The first revealed itself to me while I was in a meditative state in the early morning. The second, in Egypt, came to me in an almost trance-like state. I was told by White Eagle that this Egyptian life was important and that I was to prepare myself to relive it. For a number of sessions I would lie down on a couch and pass into what I suppose would be called a trance, in which I became very much alive in a different age, and I described all that was happening around me to the friend who was sitting by my side with pencil poised. The story was picked up time after time exactly at the point at which it had broken off in the previous session.

Another vivid experience came to me in the early hours of the morning. I was dreaming, or perhaps it is better to use the word living, in a Chinese life. I was in a pleasant Chinese house, fairly spacious, with lattice walls through which I could see into other parts of the house. I heard a tumult of voices outside the door of the house and then a heavy banging. I was momentarily frightened, but I moved forward and opened the door and, as I did so, a hand pulled me through it; outside I saw a multitude of Chinese faces all looking expectantly, almost greedily towards me. Then I felt a prick in the back of my hand which was held by the Chinese who had pulled me outside and somehow I knew that it was caused by a poisoned dart and I was facing a quick death, inflicted by the mob who were my political or religious enemies. I fell to my death gazing at the crowd of hostile faces. It was a very vivid and deeply moving soul experience. Then I saw great waves of the sea. I do not know where I was, but I heard a clear voice quite close to me say, 'And the years rolled on and on, like these rolling waves.' And with these words ringing in my ears I woke up to find myself in this day of life.

The mind has many different levels, such as the subconscious, the conscious and the super-conscious—the heavenly or spiritual mind. In meditation, the innermost spirit is striving to awaken the pupil to an awareness of itself on these many different levels. Many people now living on earth must have had countless lives, the memory of which remains in the soul. In meditation, when the deeper levels of consciousness are stirred by something the teacher, or perhaps the leader of the group, says, certain memory brain cells will be stimulated, with the result that pictures will form in what is called the imagination. These are true soul memories.

Psychologists suggest that peculiar human behaviour can be traced to events in childhood and youth and that when these memories are brought to the surface the soul sickness will be overcome and the patient cured. This is only a small aspect of the hidden cause of disturbance. The mind is complex and its subtleties little understood, and likewise the emotions which soul memories can evoke.

Every event, every thought, every emotion in the life of man is recorded on the white ether, or the akasha, hence the biblical story of the recording angel and of the soul being despatched at death to either heaven or hell. Both these states of consciousness are created not by a vengeful God, but by memories which the soul is able to read when it is freed from the physical life and has no other resort but to live in its own mind world (as we found in the last chapter.) In THE RETURN OF ARTHUR CONAN DOYLE, Sir Arthur says that when a man dies he enters into a world of his own thought creation. Similar conditions are encountered when we go into a state of deep meditation, according to what the person has established in his soul or inner self by his daily life and habitual thought. However, there is another side to this subject, and this is the mercy and love of God.

God is merciful and gives every man the chance to extricate himself from his dilemma. He sends the guardian angel and the spiritual teacher or guide to help man to find his way out of the darkness of his own creations into the Light. White Eagle says that the average individual, one who has lived a normal life of human kindness to his fellows, usually finds himself in a happy state in the spirit world, with a sense of lightness and freedom from the heaviness of physical matter; and if he is willing to listen to his guide or guardian angel he quickly comes to understand spiritual law, and his feet are set upon a path which takes him to the garden of reunion with all whom he loves.

The following example meditations show insight into past lives:

My guide led me up the white steps leading into the hall of wisdom and he took me to a small room. He went to a central table and it appeared as though he pressed some knobs and a large screen on the opposite wall lit up. I saw a wide river with small white buildings along the banks, and then some pyramids, and I knew it was a scene from Egypt. I then saw myself taking part in some sort of ceremony inside one of the buildings—it must have been a temple. Many other scenes followed, and I gathered that in some way I had betrayed the Light and had turned from the spiritual to the materialistic way of life, and suffered as a result.

I spent one meditation as an ancient Chinese pilgrim in a faded robe and leather thonged sandals, with a twisted staff, going up a winding mountain road, through trees and shrubs, with small shrines and hermits' huts at intervals, to a darkish temple of gold and red lacquer where the only light came from a shining golden Buddha.

In this example the student really relived the experience and noticed his dress and clear details. In a past life he was a poor Chinese mendicant who found the Light through the teachings of the Lord Buddha. This can also be taken at a symbolic level. The soul was shabby and seeking and expecting to find a religious teacher. He found himself walking through shrubs and trees with small shrines and huts at intervals. The shrubs and trees indicate the confused thought of lower astral and lower mental planes.

Whilst the music was being played I was in a canoe on a river. The water was sparkling and flowing swiftly and the canoe was dancing along in a joyous way; I was singing and happy. We came to an Indian camp which was my home and it was quiet and peaceful, with a tremendous feeling of security. The atmosphere was serious, but everyone went about with composure and the happiness of security.

Here the student was conscious of his emotional state; on this occasion happiness, and the atmosphere around was peaceful.

Obviously an Indian incarnation in a peaceful tribe of American Indians such as the Iroquois or the Hopis, who were known as 'the peaceful ones.'

The next scenes were extremely fluid; throngs of people in a vast building, open at one end. As I looked, a golden glow formed a radiant cross in front of it. It grew in size and splendour until it hung in the air, filling the whole place. At one time I thought I was seeing illustrations of the sun gods of the Americas, for the sky was so blue and I was standing between two carved pillars looking out from the hill into the distance.

This could have been a soul memory of an incarnation a long, long time ago, when possibly the earth's surface, and the civilisations of the day were vastly different from anything we know now. The symbol of the cross of light is the oldest symbol of the White Brotherhood. No-one can yet correctly assess the age of this planet, who were its first inhabitants or their relationship with life on other planets.

Notice in the next account how glimpses into other lives were shown reflected in the water:

🌸 I came to a very large lake with an island in the middle fringed with vegetation. I paddled across to it in a canoe. I then took a path through the woods alone. (In the boat I had not been alone.) Beyond the trees was a large clearing and in it a white square-blocked temple with unglazed apertures. Outside the building, which was white, either in blazing sunshine or it radiated its own light, were flights of steps in spiral form, having occasional platforms, but no balustrade. It was a long climb to the roof, but now I was not alone. I had a guide or teacher with me dressed in a flowing white robe. I, too, was in white—a single garment not unlike the Brotherhood robe. I was not as tall as I am today, and had medium long brown hair, slightly curly, and blue eyes, light skin, gold-painted finger and toenails, and eyelids, mouth reddened.

We rested many times on the way up, and finally reached the roof, which was flat except for an enormous central dome in the shape of a lotus, and a high parapet surrounding the entire roof.

My guide led me towards this dome and we entered through the lotus petals. Within was a small pool of crystal clear water with a small scalloped rim. I was made to lie flat on my face with my throat resting on a scallop dip. I thought it would be painful but it was not. Then I was told to look into the water. Constantly moving scenes formed and changed, and in all I saw records of past and future lives.

After a long while my guide touched my shoulder and, binding my eyes with a dark scarf, led me by the hand down the steps which we had ascended. At the bottom we parted and entered separate doors. I know I was sent to rest and recover, but how or what was within the temple I did not see.

This was long, long ago. At first I thought Maya—but it was before that, although I feel it was somewhere near South America— perhaps Atlantis.

My impression is that this was an experience of temple training in Mu.

Do not be disappointed if you only see vague, disconnected glimpses into the past. The lower mind can so easily intrude, resulting in a con- fused picture, such as in the following example:

▓ When we went back in time to earlier civilisations, I got some short disconnected pictures—brown skins, brief or scanty

clothing, but what there was, was very brightly coloured. Then I saw some sort of a ball
game, and lastly a dance. I even got some of
the movements of this; a hand clasp on every
third or fourth step, in a circle round a fire or
altar with many other people, and also nature
spirits, and something to do with sowing
seeds in spring. I don't know which civilisation I was in.

This meditation is a confused picture of the
distant past, and could be just flashes of past
incidents in different lives. I suggest that
glimmerings of memories are awakening in the
soul consciousness.

In the following example, again the contact
is vague and the student could not hold any
particular scene for more than a flash. This
very often happens to the beginner, but with
practice every scene shown can be held longer
so that even the smallest details can be ob-
served.

⬚ I became aware of a beautiful form I took
for an angel, who beckoned me and partly
opened a pair of golden gates—these were
exquisite. Here I heard the leader of the
group say that we were being taken into a
temple, and here would unfold various
scenes, some in Atlantis, which we would feel
and experience. Quite a number of scenes
flashed by, but of one I was deeply aware. I

felt that I was standing high on a rock from which I saw miles and miles of country below, and in the distance snow-tipped mountains; I felt I was up in the Andes or somewhere like that, and as I looked out upon this scene with my arms folded, I felt I was a Red Indian. Then that left me, and I was a woman on a throne in a gown of iridescent blue, with beautiful jewels. I could not place where I was. It seemed to be beyond Egypt, I felt that it was Mu; there were white walls and pillars and the woman was seated—wisdom and mercy and kindness flowed from her. It was a flash, but vivid whilst it lasted.

I think the meditator is right in believing this to have been in the continent of Mu.

I found myself in a Tibetan monastery, standing in a high stone-walled courtyard outside the entrance. Six or seven monks in orange robes took me within and up an extremely long flight of stone steps, so high that they seemed to melt into the distance. At intervals, up these steps, stood a monk or attendant. When I eventually reached the top, still supported by a monk on each side, there was a golden throne upon which sat a man in golden raiment. His head was shaven, but he wore a black head-dress similar to the Mikado; behind him hung a gold tissue curtain upon which was a large eye—staring—and it seemed as if there were many coloured rays of varying lengths instead of lashes. I was conscious of being subjected to intense questioning. What the questions were, or what answers I gave, I don't know. Neither can I remember what then happened.

This was an interesting and detailed memory but incomplete, probably due to the earthly mind putting up a barrier at the end. The all-seeing eye was of course an ancient symbol, important especially to the Egyptians.

As the meditation began we ascended a steep path, narrow and wooded, up the mountain side. At the summit we came to a flat expanse. Before us was an open-air refectory with long tables at which were seated many brothers wearing the brown habits of monks. We passed through the refectory into the chapel. Within it the world was forgotten; it fell away from the consciousness completely. The interior was vast and dim. There was no lighting yet light was there. Before the central altar knelt the twelve perfect brethren; three on each side of the altar. All was stillness and vastness, yet alive with the vibration of the great power manifesting there. Many many brethren were seated in circles round, but they appeared to be like knights. When the kneeling brethren at the altar rose and were seated before it, one of them came and fed the altar fire and it rose up as a silver column, high, silent and very brilliant.

Notice again how the student was able to absorb and retain quite a degree of detail:

I found myself on a high peak from which I could see distant mountain ranges, gold against a peach sky. I saw branches of cherry blossom and below, the valleys were filled with its whiteness. In a valley to my right stood a small white temple—circular and pillared as a Greek tholos and yet, as I went down the mountain side and approached the temple, I felt that this was Japan. The temple was now very much larger. A bell was ringing and white figures led me gently up wide white steps and drew me into the temple. Here I was greeted by a most charming Japanese person whose smile was so warm and kind. She was dressed in a pale pink kimono, with flowery designs at hem and waist, and her hair was beautifully arranged with flowers in typical Japanese fashion. She led me outside and we came upon a large group of people who were all pointing towards something I couldn't see. My companion took me by my left arm and we wandered through the gardens of the temple for some time. Snow-capped mountains surrounded us, and I saw and heard little waterfalls and streams. She showed me flowers and told me to love the flowers, to open my heart to them, to see their beauty. I wondered why we had not met before in meditation, and I believe she pointed out how difficult it was if I insisted upon being so independent! She advised me to try to be a little less 'separate.'

I am sure this was a picture of a Japanese incarnation and it was the student's guide and teacher who was telling her not to separate herself from her companions of the spirit realms— her independence was holding up her spiritual unfoldment.

This meditation clearly shows the purpose of the brief glimpse into a past life:

I gazed at a beautiful jewel and as I watched I felt that all around me and on all the surrounding peaks were countless souls watching the star. The diamond expanded and expanded and from each facet there came a fine ray of light, and as each ray touched the waiting souls they received a jewel, each different, and all shimmering in the light. To me was given an opal, full of colour and it too seemed alive. The predominant colours were blue, green and flame. It was oval in shape and I was told that I had once possessed it when in Atlantis, but had forfeited the right to wear it, but now I had won it back. I was to use it for 'the healing of souls and of the nations.'

It will be noticed that in so many of these experiences the meditator is on a high mountain. The feeling of being high up, far removed from the level of physical life, indicates a raised state of consciousness.

Humanity is very much older than has yet been calculated, and has passed through age after age during which it has experienced the early as well as more advanced stages of life and civilisation.

Many of these glimpses into past lives received in meditation refer to a very far distant past and are memories of spiritual training and teaching indelibly impressed not upon the brain but upon the soul. Sometimes, however, these soul memories can be brought to the surface of the mind by questioning when the subject has been put into a hypnotic trance. As in dreams one can receive vivid impressions which are really soul memories from a distant past rising to the surface of the mind.

XI

THE INTERPRETATION OF MEDITATIONS

Spiritual truth is often taught by means of symbols, and the true significance of a meditation experience can be missed if the student does not understand the language of symbols. As White Eagle says: 'Every initiate must learn the language of symbols and be able to interpret this language in his own soul. You may see many things in visions during your meditation, but you will only learn truth from what you see by understanding the meaning of spiritual symbols.'

In this section I am therefore giving a simple interpretation of symbols which occur most frequently in meditation. I should like to make it very clear, however, that the meaning of a symbol can vary according to the context in which it is seen, and, especially according to the soul need of the aspirant at a particular time. In spiritual matters, it is quite impossible to dot every *i* and cross every *t*, and it is unwise to try to do so. The interpretations which follow are meant to serve as a guide only. *It is not intended to establish a hard and fast rule.* Understanding will very gradually grow in the soul during the hours of meditation until the aspirant reaches the point where the symbols given speak to him clearly.

A

ARCHWAY. Passing through into something new. It may signify an initiation and apply either spiritually or to a new phase in the earthly life. One of my students frequently saw a beautiful golden archway and through it a golden haired child, but she could never get through the archway to the other side. This immediately suggests to me 'the acceptable time of the Lord.' The golden archway (which has to be built through the life) leads through into the promised land, or into a wider consciousness, but this will only come at the right time, when the soul is ready. The golden haired boy suggests to me the Christ Child, or the growing Christ consciousness.

B

BOOK. A record of activities or of lessons learnt. It could indicate that the student is learning wisdom; or it could symbolise the holy writ or spiritual law. It is a symbol sometimes used by a particular master. Here a student has herself given the interpretation of the open or closed book.

I felt my guide was speaking to me. He held a golden book in his hand. The book remained closed, though others were holding open books and I seemed to understand that I must wait until I had learned more before the book would be opened for me and I could accept the teaching it contained.

BREAD (OR CORN) AND GRAPES. The cosmic body of Christ of which we all partake. Sustenance from God. All the provision God makes for man's life in earthly form. White Eagle says: 'What is meant by the words, "I AM the bread of life...?" Those familiar with our teachings will understand that the words I AM refer to the one supreme Light, the one God, the one life, which is in all the universe. As we meditate on this, in the great silence, a new consciousness arises, a consciousness of infinity, of divinity, of eternity. We begin to realise that the I AM dwells deep in our hearts.

'*This* is the bread of life, and when we partake we know eternal life and our consciousness is illumined. Man the microcosm then becomes merged in God the macrocosm.

'The bread, the corn that feeds the body of man, is the cosmic body, the body of the sun, because the sun interpenetrates the particles of earth and brings forth corn from mother earth. Bread is produced through the provision, through the love and through the perfect law of the one supreme Being, the Great Architect of the Universe. Therefore, every mouthful we eat should be a remembrance, every meal a divine communion.'

The bread can also symbolise human experience—karma. Again, White Eagle says: 'In our communion service we interpret the bread as the symbol of human experience. When you are told to receive and eat the bread of heaven, understand that it means that you accept your karma, knowing that it is indeed your food. Your experience is the food which helps the soul and spirit to grow towards perfect manhood and womanhood.

'The wine is the juice of the grapes passed through the winepress. This again is the symbol of human experience; how man himself has to be "squeezed" and suffers either physically, emotionally, mentally or spiritually; but out of suffering is produced the most beautiful, sweet, divine essence—the essence of the love of God. This truth is presented to you in communion because this essence or wine strengthens the soul, heals the wounds made by the difficulties and disappointments of life.' (See WINE IN A GOBLET.)

C

CANDLE. A lighted candle symbolises the Christ Spirit which is in the heart of everyman. Seen in meditation, it probably indicates all that is good, pure and of the spirit as opposed to materialism. It is also a symbol associated with one of the elder brethren. Meditation on the still, white flame can be very helpful.

CARVING OR CARVED WALLS. Decoration or lily-work—the finishing off of a piece of work. It could mean that the meditator is too much concerned with detail and cannot see the whole picture, or it could mean that more work is yet to be done, either physically or spiritually.

CAVE OR TUNNEL, WITH LIGHT AT THE END. This could indicate the need for patience, and suggests to me there are problems and difficulties to be solved, but in the end everything will be overcome and a state of great happiness will be achieved.

CENSER, SILVER. This signifies opportunity or the tool given to the pupil to work for the Master of the Great White Lodge. Censing is a method of purification. To see a censer might therefore indicate a work of cleansing or purifying, or even healing. Or it could refer to the work of the Brotherhood in the temple.

CHEQUERED FLOOR, BLACK AND WHITE. A masonic symbol representing the positive and negative forces. The neophyte has to learn to discern between white and black, good and evil, or in other words he has to learn to get his values right and true and find balance, equilibrium.

CHESS, GAME OF. The eternal battle between good and evil, light and darkness. It also symbolises the divine plan, and the order which lies behind even so-called chance happenings on the earth plane—the game is played by the Master Mind, God.

CHILDREN, BEING WITH. This signifies someone who is young in heart and indicates a spiritual quality of joy, happiness and freedom. It is always good to be with children in meditation as this also indicates the influence of the divine Mother spirit.

CINEMA SCREEN. A large screen on a wall upon which pictures appear is often seen in meditation. This is a symbol of the akashic records; often people see their life's record as on a film; sometimes glimpses of past lives may also be shown. (See MIRROR.)

CIRCLE OF LIGHT. God's all enfolding, eternal love.

CLIMBING STEPS. See STEPS, CLIMBING.

CLOAK. Either protection or something that is being hidden. In the following example meditation, the student is given the protection of the pure white cloak of spirit, and this is then hidden by the brown cloak of the earthly life:

> ▓ I realised that we were back in the class and became deeply aware of a beautiful peaceful presence standing in the centre. I felt now as if someone had placed a most lovely cloak around me. It was of pure white and shimmered, with a golden clasp inset with an amethyst at its neck and collar. Another cloak was put over this one, and this was brown, like those worn by monks over their white habits.

CLOSED GATE. See GATE, CLOSED.

COLOURS. When the colour is pure and clear it indicates certain qualities, as listed below. But if it becomes heavy, tinged with black or brown, the quality is being coloured by the lower nature. For instance, the rose red of pure love can become the murky dark red of passion, selfishness and sensuality; or the yellow ray of the highest spiritual mind can become darkened by material thought and the earthly mind.

Red. The colour of love and life, the life of the nervous system. It is used in healing to give vitality. Pure pink or true rose colour indicates selfless love.

Orange and yellow. The yellow ray is that of the highest spiritual mind—divine intelligence.

Green. The soothing colour of nature. It indicates adaptability, sympathy and harmony.

Blue. Indicates healing, devotion and aspiration.

Violet. The colour of the seventh ray of white magic and ceremonial.

Gold. The Christ Light and love—the sun.

Silver. Linked with the moon and the Mother and has a cleansing and purifying effect.

White and black. The two opposites—positive and negative, good and evil, day and night, etc.

CORN, EAR OF. See BREAD.

COUNCIL CHAMBER. This signifies the outworking of the divine law behind all life. Every event is part of the great plan which God holds for the evolution of life. There is a group of great masters who watch over, guide and protect humanity, within the Christ Star Circle.

CROOK, SHEPHERD's. Symbolic of the shepherd, who guides, leads and cares for those in need:

🌼 I stood waiting rather uncertainly on the steps of the golden temple, and felt unable to enter it, when I caught sight of a number of tools and implements leaning agains a pillar. I realised they were the symbols of the ways different people would take in their particular work. My attention was held by a shepherd's crook, and I longed to be a shepherd and bring healing and comfort to those in need. I was allowed to look into the temple and see a vision of what I would aspire to become: I saw a young radiant figure in a shimmering robe and with a crook in his hand, walking through the streets of a city of light; wherever he went he was followed by people who had come into the city to seek help, guidance, or healing. Those who followed him were recharged by the virtue that went out from him.

CROSS. This well-known symbol indicates the tests and trials of the soul incarnated on earth and is frequently seen in meditation—

🌼 I became conscious of a figure (which was not Jesus) hanging darkly and limply on a cross. It stood out desolate, forlorn and alone. It was behind me and behind the kneeling multitude—it was past and done with.

This was a symbol of having passed through an experience or a spiritual test, which could be likened to a crucifixion of the soul. Again—

🌼 My heart reached outward and upward to

the golden mountains. The topmost peak was in the shape of a perfect, equal-sided triangle of pure golden light. I passed through its centre and on the other side saw a cross with a crucified figure stretched upon it. The atmosphere was heavy and dark and all life had left the figure on the cross; it was slumped and broken. For a split second I wanted to recoil from it, but I didn't move. Compassion stirred in my heart and, as it did so, a beam of light passed through me. It touched the figure on the cross and a new life and a new hope stirred within, so that it gradually became a radiant, living, vibrating form with arms outstretched to love and to bless.

This meditation shows how, through suffering and crucifixion, divine love and compassion are born in the heart, to be poured out in service to others. The rose of divine love blooms on the cross.

CROSS WITH ROSE AT CENTRE. The transformation of the cross of sacrifice. (See foregoing interpretation.)

CROWN BEING PLACED ON HEAD. A ruler, or one who has triumphed or will triumph over weakness.

CUP, GRAIL. See GRAIL CUP.

D

DANCING. Conveys joy and celebration, related to others or to oneself.

DIAMOND. The jewel which contains all the

colours of the spectrum. It signifies the pure spirit. The diamond shape is made up of two triangles (the trinity). Thus whereas the six-pointed star, made up of two triangles which are interlocked, symbolises man made perfect through earthly experience, the diamond symbolises the pure heavenly spirit before it becomes an individual—a spiritual atom, the very beginning of life. To be within the diamond can symbolise the consciousness of God which brings perfect happiness and peace.

As I contemplated the lotus and looked upon it, I saw the golden stamens, all so pure and perfect, and gradually the diamond appeared. Oh, the beauty of this exquisite jewel! It seemed that there were no facets: it was not the hard cut diamond of earth, but was like a dewdrop, so very pure and perfect; and as the sunlight shone through it all the pure colours of the spectrum or rainbow rayed out from this diamond, which became a pulsating living thing; that is the only way I can describe it!

DOVES, BLACK AND WHITE. The need to learn the valuable lesson of equilibrium or balance. Balancing of the opposite forces of white and black, good and evil, is one of the lessons to be learnt on the spiritual path.

DOVE, WHITE, WITH RUBY IN BEAK. A sign of both peace and love. The white dove (peace) brings in its beak the red ruby, symbol of the love, friendship and goodwill in the heart. (See RUBIES.)

DRAGON, BEING SLAIN BY KNIGHT. A dragon signifies the lower nature. The knight slaying the dragon symbolises the constant combat between good and evil, and the eventual over-coming of evil by the power of good.

E

EAGLE. The white eagle means a spiritual teacher. It is also the symbol of St. John, and the Age of Aquarius. A flying eagle indi-cates release of the higher mind from earthly bondage.

   I ran towards some white horses, jump-ed on one of them and galloped into the sun. The horse grew wings which became those of an eagle, and then I was the eagle, soaring above the empyrean, free—free of all physical ties.

This meditation indicates the higher mind and purest intellect which, when set free from the bondage of the earthly mind, can soar as on wings to the heights of spiritual truth.

EYE (LOOKING AT EVERYTHING). Usually a symbol of God's watchfulness over humanity. It is often referred to as the all-seeing eye and was one of the symbols frequently used in Egypt.

🌸 I saw a single eye shining from the centre of an immense pale gold Buddha-like figure which seemed to fill the sky. From the eye light streamed out on to a great land of green and yellow fields. A feeling of great love came from this light. I was absorbed by this single eye of love. I was standing in a place of perfect golden light, I felt I was in the Star; the single eye blazed at its centre.

F

FALLING, FEELING OF. See FEAR.

FAWN. A shy retiring nature. This symbol probably appears to teach the student not to be too shy to take up the opportunities which lie ahead for spiritual development.

FEAR. One of the first lessons that has to be learnt on the astral plane is that of overcoming fear, and of knowing with complete certainty that nothing can hurt one physically. In the spirit world one has no physical body. A student might be given the test of flinging himself down from a great height, or of an encounter with a wild animal (see LION). One student told me how she saw a very large spider's web and, although normally very fearful of spiders, she felt no fear in this case. (See SPIDER'S WEB.) Another said:

🌸 I saw in front of me two gold pillars with pointed tops; on these points was placed a rounded arch, and between them a wooden door, marked 'HAVE COURAGE'. I wondered what was on the other side of that doorway and opened it to look. I found that, having done so, I could not retreat but saw in front of me an enveloping deep blue midnight sky full of stars and golden planets. I began to move freely among them in space but without touching them. Then I was afraid as I was all alone and did not land anywhere but kept on travelling. As soon as I felt fear I began to fall—and fell and fell and fell, never landing or touching anywhere. I became panic-stricken. Then a lovely white bird with a red rose in its beak came to me and offered me the rose. The relief was immense, and by some magnetic attraction I was enabled to follow the flight of this bird, which finally placed me in front of three kings seated on three golden thrones, with gold crowns on their heads and dressed in glistening white garments. The centre king of the three was seated higher than the others and was altogether loftier. He stepped down from his throne and, placing his sceptre upon my head, gave me a harmless serpent. 'Be wise and understanding,' he said. The king at his right hand then stepped down and placed his sword upon my head. He gave me a little lamb, saying, 'Be pure and tender and white like this innocent little lamb.' The king at his left hand placed his sword upon my head and gave me a sword to hold, and said, 'Fight a good fight for the Light.'

Symbols to notice particularly here are the white bird, symbol of a spiritual teacher; the red rose, symbol of that perfect love which takes away fear; being touched three times by the sceptre or sword of a king: the king indicates an illumined teacher, and the sword touching the head indicates triumph over a particular weakness, in this case fear. In this meditation the touching of the head is accompanied each time by an exhortation—a reminder of the lesson to be learned and remembered, following triumph over the weakness.

FEET, BARE. The simple trusting in God, the foundation upon which to build a spiritual life. You must walk the path with bare feet and endure the stones and the rough places of life as well as enjoying the soft mossy places which come in between the stones.

FEET WEARING GOLDEN SANDALS. Feet signify understanding, and to see feet clothed in gold means the wearer is someone who has a true understanding of spiritual values. Beautiful feet illustrate good understanding, a sound foundation.

FLOWERS. See also individual interpretation of RED, WHITE and GOLD ROSES, VIOLETS. Flowers collectively indicate the sweetness of nature, mother earth, the divine Mother. The following meditation interprets two flowers often seen in meditation:

The Christ stood before us with His hands outstretched to us—in one hand was a pure white lily and in the other a deep, deep red rose with a glorious scent. He told us that the white lily symbolised the pure heavenly spirit waiting to be born upon the earth plane. The deep red rose was the earthly being waiting to be born on the spirit plane, bringing with it all the wisdom and experience it had gained upon earth.

G

GATE, CLOSED. The earthly mind barring the way to spiritual understanding. The soul's karma may be the gate which is barring the way. Patience is needed for there are karmic debts to be paid and lessons to be learnt before any advance is made.

GOBLET OF WINE. See under WINE IN GOBLET.

GRAIL CUP. The cup of communion, symbol of more glorious life. A centre or receptacle of spiritual power and light. The heart centre is often likened to a grail cup because it is the human receptacle of divine love. There are certain places on the earth where a grail cup is to be seen clairvoyantly; these centres are filled with spiritual light, and a sensitive person can feel the power which has been concentrated there either by the work and ritual of an ancient religion or possibly by the life of a holy and sainted soul.

GRAPES. (See also under WINE.) The pressing of the juice from the grapes symbolises the way in which, through pain and suffering (the wine-press), divine love (the wine) is produced in man's heart. The wine is the divine essence, the Christ love.

H

HANDS. The interpretation would depend on the circumstances and soul need of the aspirant. Generally indicates a helping hand, either being extended to the aspirant, or an injunction to *give* a helping hand.

HAND WITH RING. A means of identification. It could refer to a certain great master who is often recognised by an amethyst ring. Interpretation could also depend upon the finger on which the ring is worn. It could mean a certain high office or degree of initiation.

HEIGHT, LOOKING DOWN FROM. An elevated state of consciousness in the astral body enabling the spirit to look down upon the material world and learn valuable lessons from this higher level.

HORSE, WHITE, RIDDEN BY KNIGHT. See under KNIGHT.

HORSE, WINGED. Like the symbol of the eagle, indicates the higher mind which when set free from the bondage of the narrow earthly mind can soar as on wings to the heights of spiritual truth.

HORSESHOE. Traditional symbol of good or ill fortune; when seen in meditation, promises a helping hand in time of trouble from the guide or teacher who is in charge of the pupil. You must have faith, and trust in God's love and wisdom.

HOURGLASS. Probably the need for release from the earthly consciousness and bondage of time and the realisation of the timelessness of eternity. Time is a creation of the earthly mind and life. In spirit there is no time—one lives in the eternal now.

J

JEWELS. Indicate different aspects of spiritual truth. See individual interpretations for DIAMOND, PEARL, RUBY.

K

KEYS AND KEYHOLE, GOLDEN. The key to the inner kingdom or to the golden world of God. In the mystery schools of the past, the question was sometimes asked of the candidate to a higher degree, 'Where lies the key?' The answer was, 'In the heart.' The golden city is a state of consciousness which lies deep within the heart and the gate to it is unlocked by love and selfless loving service.

KEYS, BUNCH OF (SEVEN). The many different ways or paths to the truth, or many doors to unlock before passing into the centre of the temple; many experiences to undergo before attaining the perfect life.

KING, CROWNED WITH GOLD. One who has triumphed over spiritual weakness, or it could indicate a coming triumph.

KNIGHT IN SHINING ARMOUR. A spiritual leader, one who has overcome the tests of the physical life; or possibly the aspirant's own higher self.

KNIGHT ON A WHITE HORSE. A symbol of the Master, or the great spiritual leader of the new age of brotherhood and of the evolving spiritual and higher psychic powers in man. In the following meditation a student contacted the Master of the seventh ray who is leading us into the new Age of Aquarius. The star he carried is to guide us and the babe symbolises the new age now being born:

> We were following a great white charger on which sat a beautiful figure wearing a deep violet cloak; in his right hand he held high a gleaming golden star and in his left arm he held a little baby.

L

LADDER REACHING TO THE SKY. The bridge which can be built between the earthly and spiritual state of consciousness.

LAKE WITH SWAN. See SWAN ON PEACEFUL LAKE.

LAMB WITH SHEPHERD. See CROOK.

LAMP, LIGHTED. See CANDLE.

LIGHT, CIRCLE OF. See CIRCLE.

LIGHT, AT END OF CAVE OR TUNNEL. See CAVE.

LIGHTHOUSE. Shows the way which will lead to spiritual unfoldment and safe harbour after the battering of the rough seas of life.

LILIES. Purity—the pure heavenly spirit. They also draw attention to divine Mother. Their perfume is associated with one of the elder brethren.

LILY POOL. The still centre ... peace. See Chapter V, THE LOTUS POOL AND THE ELDER BRETHREN.

LION. An animal of immense strength, the 'king of the beasts.' A friendly lion seen in meditation could indicate the immense strength and help which always comes to us from God in times of great need. A fierce lion could indicate the need to overcome fear (see FEAR). Having summoned the required courage to pass the lion, it would then become harmless.

M

MIRROR. A method often used by a spiritual teacher is to lead the pupil to a mirror to see a reflection of its true self or the particular spiritual degree at which it has arrived. It could also be part of a glimpse into past lives; looking in a mirror and seeing oneself in the clothes of another age is quite a common occurrence in meditation. See also under CINEMA SCREEN and Chapter X, INSIGHT INTO PAST LIVES.

MOUNTAIN, BEING ON TOP OF. See HEIGHT.

MUSIC. As the sense of hearing begins to develop in the soul body, the aspirant will hear music during meditation. This often happens in the temple where the music expresses the perfect harmony the soul feels. Sometimes the music heard is the harmony of the spheres; this helps to convey to the soul an idea of the vastness of God's creation, and gives it an assurance of the wonderful plan and order which is the divine law of all life. A particular piece of music can also be used to convey an idea, place or person the meditator especially associates with it.

N
NATURE SPIRITS. These are often seen in meditation and demonstrate their role in the great scheme of life. A student writes:

> Suddenly a little gnome friend darted along to me carrying a large, dazzling white jewel which he was busy polishing. As the happiness of seeing him flashed through me I was for a fleeting moment back in the temple; but now, set in the middle of the front of the altar, was a great jewel in the shape of a six-pointed star. I knew my little gnome friend was connected in some way with putting the jewel there, and in realising it I was conscious too of the interrelationship of all creation on all planes in all kingdoms.

This is a very good meditation. The little gnome was a very real friend in spirit who was helping the student in her work of spiritualising her life on all planes.

O
OPEN BOOK. See under BOOK.
OWL. Wisdom; also silent watchfulness. Keep quiet, be patient and you will receive in your heart the communication from spirit.

P

PATH, WALKING ALONG. The evolutionary path
along which every soul has to journey; sometimes the way is difficult with many tests and
trials, at other times it is easier and the soul can
look back and see how far it has journeyed and
the reasons for its suffering. Two interesting
examples:

    ※ I was climbing up a steep circular path,
very narrow, that wound upwards like a
corkscrew with no visible means of support.
Eventually I got to the top and at the very
tip was the cross within the circle with the
rose at its centre. It was upright, and seemed
to be a doorway and I knew that if I could
get through it I would enter eternity, or the
sky. I cannot explain it as there appeared to
be nothing on the other side, but I knew it
represented everything. (See CROSS WITH
ROSE AT CENTRE).

    I was walking up a mountain pathway.
The sky was blue and cloudless, the air in-
vigorating and there were many wild flowers
beside the path and on the hillsides. I felt
free and happy and gay. Eventually I came
to a cave and entered it. Opposite the entrance and to the left and right benches had
been cut out of the rock. To all outward
appearances the cave was deserted, dark and
dismal, yet I felt there was more there than
I could see. I waited for a while, but nothing
changed; it was as though a shutter was

down, so I decided I had better make my way to the lily pool and restart my meditation from there.

This last is particularly interesting. So often in life a curtain seems to be drawn before our eyes and we cannot see the meaning of what is happening, but we just have to keep on keeping on along the pathway of life. Eventually we see our way clearly, but until we do we have to keep returning to that still centre within (the lily pool) and we are sustained and helped forward.

PEARLS. A particular facet of spiritual truth. The pearl of great price buried within the unprepossessing oyster shell—the inner spiritual reward which comes after great suffering, self-sacrifice or service to others. Following the path which appears unattractive, but one knows it is the right one to take, can lead to a hidden jewel of happiness. The pearl could also indicate the pearl healing ray.

I saw that every lily appearing on the calm water produced a pearl as it opened, denoting one of the great virtues. These were collected by bright winged fairies who handed them over to the little children playing around the pool. The children loved them, made pictures with them and handed them to the winged beings looking after them. These in turn gently scattered them among the earth people. Some caught them

in their hands and meditated lovingly upon
them; others dropped them. Yet others
picked them up and cherished them. And as
the pearls were multiplied by the lilies of the
pool and finally reached more and more
earth people, these began to value them
more widely, so that the earth-plane itself
became more and more beautiful, holy and
virtuous; and darkness, ignorance and the
cardinal sins gradually faded out.

The pearl reflects all seven colours of the
spectrum. Thus each must make what he can
of the gifts he is given.

PILLARS. Tall upright pillars indicate the perfect man, with feet firmly on earth, aspiring to
God. Two pillars at an entrance indicate the
positive and negative aspects in all life. The
twelve pillars of a circular temple could indicate the twelve signs of the zodiac, or the twelve
great evolutionary ages of man.

R

RING ON HAND. See HAND WITH RING.

ROSES, GOLD, PINK, RED, WHITE. The rose is
always a symbol of love. A gold rose is often
associated with the master of the new age. It
also indicates golden sunlight and its warming
and softening influence on the brilliant
earthly mind.

A pink rose is particularly associated with
divine Mother and also with the Christ love in
the human heart.

A red rose is indicative of deep human love, attained through suffering and experience. This symbol is frequently shown by one who wishes to convey this particular human love to the recipient.

A white rose, often single or in the shape of a Christmas rose, can be interpreted as purity of life and thought—the pure spirit. It is also a symbol of pure, divine love.

RUBIES. Brotherly love; goodwill and fidelity. (See DOVE WITH RUBY IN BEAK.)

RUNNING AWAY. Fear and the necessity to overcome some physical or spiritual weakness. See FEAR.

S

SANDALS, GOLD. See FEET WEARING GOLDEN SANDALS.

SCALES, PAIR OF. The divine law of equilibrium.

> I felt the presence of our masters and saw on the little altar a pair of scales. The masters came forward and put a small sack of equal weight on either side of the scales so that they balanced equally. In one sack was a heart and in the other a head.

This points out that the influence of the mind and the heart should be perfectly balanced in man's life.

SCEPTRE BEING PUT IN HAND. A ruler. It could mean extra responsibilities being given to the recipient, as well as the strength and power needed for the task.

SEA, BEING NEAR OR IMMERSED IN. See WATER.

SEESAW. Like a pair of scales (see above), indicates the need for balance in the life and for the aspirant to learn the law of equilibrium.

SHEPHERD WITH LAMB AND CROOK. See CROOK, SHEPHERD'S.

SILVER CENSER. See CENSER, SILVER.

SPIDER'S WEB. Suggests life within the divine plan; all the intricate lines or threads lead or build up into the centre, each thread growing out of another and helping to hold the whole together, and each necessary to the whole pattern. The picture might be given to teach the aspirant that every happening in his life, however irksome or however apparently trivial, should be accepted as part of the divine plan, and as leading to further development. It should give him the confidence to keep on keeping on.

In the example meditation there is a diamond instead of a spider at the centre of the web, indicating the happiness which results when a weakness is conquered:

I was taken and shown the flowers and insects, then all of a sudden there appeared in the sunlight a colossal spider's web, suspended in the light. I have a horror of spiders and anticipated seeing the creature but the web was so silken and glistening in colour, and in the centre was a most beautiful diamond; it reflected the light and all the colours in the rainbow.

SNOWDROPS. Purity, new life, after a period of darkness and suffering.

STAR. I think all White Eagle students are familiar with the symbol of the star. The six-pointed star is the symbol of man made perfect. Here is an interesting meditation:

> I saw a multi-coloured star on the site of New Lands building,* and shooting out from each point were other small stars, and they fell in places all round the earth. I was taken to watch one grow—and they all did, until they all united to form a glowing mass, a golden globe of earth. Gradually, out of this, grew multitudes of perfected forms of mankind, creating endlessly in tremendous activity—creating, creating, creating patterns, colours and tones. The atmosphere of kindness, brotherliness, helpfulness and love was almost overwhelming.

STEPS, CLIMBING MANY. This indicates the soul's journey along the evolutionary path (see PATH). Steps must always be climbed with courage and determination until the goal is reached.

> Then I became aware of being in a temple. Here were the elders, men of real wisdom, wearing pure white robes, with a gold circlet, which had a snake's head en-

* Refers to the new Temple of the White Eagle Lodge in Hampshire.

graved upon it, upon their brows. They were all seated around the table and they had maps and plans; then I saw a most beautiful scroll. (see COUNCIL CHAMBER). I heard the leader's voice describing the temple and the many, many steps we were to walk up to the top. It was strange; I felt as if I had walked them before. At one point I fell, but got up and walked up them again. This time there were many, many more steps, but on reaching the top, oh, the unutterable peace, the gentle love, and the ineffable light.

Many meditations give glimpses of past lives. For instance, the above description of the temple and the many steps could be a flash of memory in the soul of a past vivid experience such as climbing the countless steps of an ancient Mayan temple, or possibly an Atlantean temple. Meditation can touch secret chords in the soul, memories of actual happenings at some time in a long, long life. Or the above could be a spiritual symbol of a soul's experience climbing the steps towards heaven.

STEPS LEADING TO WHITE DOOR. Steps which are before the candidate and which, if taken patiently and earnestly, lead to the door of initiation into heavenly mysteries.

STONE, POLISHED. A stone is a symbol well known to the ancient Brotherhood. Every soul is like a rough stone or ashlar, which has to be polished to perfection during physical life before it is ready to take its place in the temple. If the pupil is presented with a polished stone, it means encouragement to get on with the job, and to keep on keeping on, and the result will be attainment of perfection.

SUN. The symbol of God, the creative force behind all life.

> I stood on a sea of molten gold, which extended as far as the eye could see. On the far horizon blazed a vast sun of white fire. I was robed in white with a golden girdle round my waist and golden sandals on my feet and I was veiled. I felt very small and alone on the mighty sea, but I knew that somehow I must reach the sun, so I began to walk across the waters. After a while I realised that I was not alone but that on either side of me, stretching right up to and into the sun, were angel beings helping me and encouraging me. They seemed to close their ranks behind me, bearing me forward nearer and nearer to the sun, until I was caught up into its white fire.

SWAN ON PEACEFUL LAKE. The swan is a symbol of an initiate, or initiation. The peaceful lake indicates the quiet waters of the soul, unruffled by emotion—a necessary preliminary to initiation.

T

TEMPLE. See Chapter VI. THE TEMPLE OF COMMUNION.

TREE IN BLOSSOM. The promise of fruition.

TREES. A beautiful single tree is a symbol of the pulsating life-force or the life of God in all realms. The ancient brothers believed and taught their followers that the tree symbolised the life-forces and spiritual powers which lived in man and from which man could draw sustenance. The roots represented the earthly forces and powers which sustain the physical body, and the branches the cosmic and spiritual powers which can be drawn upon to sustain the soul and spirit.

Sometimes the aspirant is taken to a temple of nature where tall trees form the pillars and green branches the roof. The aspirant will derive strength in meditation from standing or sitting with his back against a tree. He will also feel that he is growing with the tree, or being pulled upwards to heaven. (White Eagle has often advised us, when feeling depleted of life-force, to find a tree on the earth plane and stand with spine against its trunk, breathing in the life-force which can be felt pulsating through the tree. This is very potent and healing.) Seeing a tree could be a promise of strength and help.

TREES, BEING SURROUNDED BY. Indicates the earthly mind with the true vision obscured by the intellect. 'Unable to see the wood for the trees' describes this experience.

TRUMPET. We read in the Bible that 'the trumpet shall sound and the dead shall be raised, incorruptible, and we shall all be changed.' This conception is unacceptable to the thinking mind today, but when interpreted in the spiritual sense of a heavenly sound or a heavenly call or proclamation which strikes a responsive chord in the soul, awakening it to spiritual truth and reality, the biblical language takes on more meaning. The words of Ecclesiastes, 'the dead know not anything,' refer not to the physically dead but to the dead in spirit who know nothing of the reality of eternal life. Thus the trumpet could be a 'trumpet sounding in the soul'—an awakening, a quickening. It could herald a breakthrough into wider consciousness. It also suggests praise and jubilation.

TUNNEL OR CAVE WITH LIGHT AT END. See under CAVE.

V

VIOLETS. I always accept this as a symbol of the master of the violet ray, the seventh ray of the higher psychic power. In meditation our attention is often drawn first to the fragrance.

W

WALKING ALONG PATH. See PATH.

WALLED GARDEN, WALKING IN. This is a symbol of the infinite and eternal garden; it could indicate a desire for or the promise of protection.

WALLS, CARVED. See CARVING.

WATER, WATERMILL, BEING NEAR. Cleansing, purifying, healing. Water is the symbol of the soul or psyche and of the emotional nature. If it is clear, pure running water or a waterfall, it signifies that the soul is being cleansed by the waters of the spirit; in order to pass the water initiation it is necessary to gain mastery over the emotions. This is illustrated in the story of Jesus walking on the water: when Peter stepped out of the boat to walk towards Jesus all went well until the disciple suddenly doubted, the emotion of fear swept through him and he started to sink. In other words, his emotions overwhelmed him.

WINDOW, LIGHTED, IN DARK HOUSE. See LIGHT-HOUSE.

WINE IN GOBLET. Wine is, of course, one of the communion symbols and indicates the divine essence of love, the Christ Spirit which is within and sustaining all life.

WINGED DISC. One of the symbols in use in the Greek and Egyptian mysteries. The disc is the symbol of man's heart centre, like the golden sun, and the wings attached are the wings of his soul which, when he has learnt to use them, will enable him to fly into the higher worlds.

WRITING IN BOOK. See BOOK.

WRITING ON SANDSTONE. Indicates that the soul is overcoming suffering which is in the past and karma is being worked through.

XII

ADVANCED MEDITATION

White Eagle tells us:

'When you meditate you should focus your whole attention upon God, upon the manifestation of God in form. Thus you will create for yourselves the perfect form, the Perfect One. In that Perfect One your higher self will manifest. As you feel love for your fellows and love for all life, you will find your aura expanding until you are wholly consumed with love, and all thought of self dies. Then you will realise that divine ecstasy which is the goal of mystics and saints of all time. The joy the aspirant experiences in true meditation is beyond anything which man can gain from ordinary mental and material pursuits.

'Cease from all conflict; seek only the kingdom of God, the being of pure love. There, in the holy presence of God, you will find all truth. This is the first essential if you wish to advance on the path of discipleship. It is the golden secret and must be put into practice continually otherwise the secret will evade you and you will be enveloped in material things. By practising the secret of soul harmony you will start to change the atoms of your physical, mental, etheric and celestial bodies.

'It is not enough to know truth intellectually for this is to hold stones in your hand. The wise man becomes his knowledge, and his whole being is truth and beauty. Thus he becomes master over himself and his kingdom.'

This then is our goal in meditation, and to help all my students find the golden secret White Eagle describes, I am now including some examples of meditations received by students who have followed White Eagle's teaching and methods faithfully for some years and achieved a fair degree of progress in meditation.

If you are a beginner, don't be daunted and give up, thinking meditation is not for you because you do not as yet have clear and detailed experiences in your meditation as are described here. Some people have no difficulty at all from the start, others need a good deal of practice and much patience before they can begin to experience the deepest blessing of meditation. I have had students who 'did nothing' for class after class but eventually, with perseverance, their vision was opened.

Never overlook the seemingly trivial because it could be important and mean much more to you when you have advanced a little more on the path. For instance, one of my pupils could only see one petal of a flower, probably a petal of the lotus. This seemingly unimportant thing was really significant because it symbolised the beginning of the development of a spiritual power within.

What will help you most of all to break through this barrier of blankness are your feelings of worship and thankfulness. Try to cultivate a feeling of love and thankfulness for all the gifts of life—the gift of beauty, the gifts of love and friendship, and all the bounty of nature. This love and worship will begin to create light—sunlight for you in your inner world—and it is from this light that all your future experiences in meditation will be built.

I visualised a deep valley with steep purple mountains on either side and a little sighing stream running down its centre. Our group walked beside this stream following it to its source. Here we found ourselves on the top of a mountain crowned by a huge circular white temple with alabaster columns surrounding it, and in its centre a little fountain which was the source of our stream. Behind the fountain stood a white glistening altar with many bits of paper lying on top of it. Behind the altar stood the glorious white figure of the Christ, with hands extended in blessing upon the altar. As we watched, standing around the little fountain, we saw Christ beckon with his hands, and immediately a host of great white-winged angels descended, and each took up a bit of paper from the altar and held it to his heart. We were astonished to see the papers gradually take the form of the person named upon it, and become completely healed and whole in spirit and body.

In gratitude for their healing, these folk came among our group to give us healing too, where there was physical ill the body became cured of disease. Where there was emotional trouble we were encouraged to talk and unburden, and were helped with advice. Where there was unbelief or soul-trouble, the soul was made whole and full of faith.

In all my meditation classes I direct my students to send forth the light of healing the sick in mind and body. Absent healing is one of the finest ways of being trained in the practice of meditation. To desire to help others, to pour out soul power and Light to save mankind is to develop the white magic of love within one's own heart. In the silence and tranquillity of the innermost spirit the steady work of spiritual unfoldment goes on until the moment comes when one can realise the gifts of the spirit with which God has endowed all mankind.

I was drawn right up into the Star and remained in the heart of the flame in a state of absolute stillness for some time. Then everything became as real and vivid as the physical world—it was solid, not nebulous at all. I found myself on a high and grassy hill, rather like the downs or the dales—all around was a wonderful view, but what I was most conscious of was the great oak tree under which I was standing. It was a lovely symmetrical shape, very large, sturdy and absolutely full of acorns.

Then I realised that such a dear man was standing with me—strong and sturdy like the oak, with such a kind, round, bearded face. I seemed to know him very well, as if he were a combination of all the people most dear to me. Such comfort and great love filled my heart that tears were running from my eyes because of this intense feeling of love and joy. I got the feeling that I was in the company of Pythagoras (but later, when I came upon a portrait of Apollonius of Tyana I wondered if this were he, as it reminded me of my friend in this meditation). He put into my hands a strong stout staff, which gave me such a feeling of confidence, which seems to have remained with me, for now whenever life seems too difficult and pressurised I just think of my friend and the staff and feel ready for anything.

This is an excellent illustration of the truth which the White Brotherhood is helping us to understand. It is confusing when names are given of any particular master because each one has incarnated many times, and the special personality which presents itself to you in a meditation is the life in which you were very close to him, probably as an earthly pupil in his school. The one described here could equally well be Pythagoras or Apollonius of Tyana.

From the apex of the golden triangle we went into a vertical tunnel, the walls seemed to me made of a shimmering golden transparent net substance. We rose in this 'tunnel.' At first, looking through the net, I saw clear water, and swimming in it a huge fish and then tiny tropical angel fish, beautifully coloured. As we rose higher the water gave place to green earth and growing from it a lovely tall white lily and near the ground a tiny blue speedwell, with bees and insects. We seemed to rise higher still, and then we saw a small, so white, lamb. Higher still we rose, and radiant forms appeared, and then the tunnel opened to a golden spiral path up which we rose; climbed is too arduous a word. At the top of this golden spiral was a golden star. We entered the centre of this, to be in a golden temple, with golden pillars, and at the far end a blazing golden altar, before which stood a figure with outstretched arms.

As I listened to this description of a meditation, I thought of the big fish as symbolising the passing Age of Pisces, and the clear water representing purified emotions, and the strength and balance of the human soul. As the meditator rose higher in the water, it meant the mastering of the Piscean characteristics and the emerging into the new Age of Aquarius. It went on to illustrate the gradual at-one-ment of creation in the nature and animal kingdoms; and then 'the tunnel opened to a golden spiral up which we rose into the golden star.' This was the Golden Lodge of the Christ Star Brotherhood, the goal of all man's aspiration.

After the usual heavenly contact at the beginning, I was meditating on the golden heart of the lotus and then found myself going deeper and deeper into the heart, and right down, down to the roots. I felt utterly calm, steady and still, and then became conscious of the great snake moving there—so clear, definite and real. I could see diamond shaped, bright markings on its scaly skin. I was not perturbed or bothered, but kept quite steady and aloof as it slowly spiralled upwards. In a way it was quite a friendly creature, but I felt a sense of its enormous hidden power. It spiralled up to a certain level, which somehow I recognised as the heart centre, and then the situation changed, and it was as if the snake were just below the surface of the ocean, churning up a great flood. Although very aware of this, I seemed to be quite unmoved and conscious of the fact that I and the other meditators in the group were in a little ark—on the surface of the waters, held safely in a great ray of power which I could not see, but felt. It made me think of Jesus walking on the water.

I somehow couldn't get enough light—I was praying and reaching out to God, and continually holding the whole condition strongly in the heart of the cross within the circle. But although flashes of bright pure sunlight came from my heart spasmodically, it was a struggle, like the sun rising in a misty, stormy dawn. Usually I have no difficulty at all in being at the heart of the sun and radiating light, but it was a strong steady battle to even strike these fitful bursts of brilliance. I prayed hard for light, and begged White Eagle to help. As I prayed and asked for help, I began to feel myself at the centre of a great equal-sided cross—stretched out on it, but with the light beginning to grow stronger.

Then, thank God, I was suddenly free from it all and we were in the garden, with Jesus and the masters. I knew we were all being given a deep red rose—it was drenched with rain and the thorns were very sharp, but gradually the exquisite fragrance enveloped us all with the sweetness and comfort and strength from the Brotherhood.

I think all the group were drawn into this 'rose' consciousness in the rain-drenched garden, and then suddenly a bright ray of glorious sunshine turned all the dewdrops into jewels, and everywhere there was light and birdsong—the angels of joy were lifting us to the sun.

It was an extraordinary meditation—I have never had such a real, deep and in some ways exhausting spiritual experience. Comparing meditations with the others in the group was interesting. A number of the others had come, very much in turmoil with material emotional problems. One, for example, had been very upset before coming by hearing on the news the wife of one of the hostages in a hijacking episode, and was praying to be able to help them. These people found it difficult to get away at first, but most of them managed to 'get there' in the end.

Another to her astonishment got the Ark of the Covenant in some way containing the light of the lotus, and a great feeling of protection. One or two found themselves going up a spiral staircase made of crystal (my diamond studded snake spiralling). All got a great sense of peace and protection. All got the wave of joy at the end. Could this strange meditation be something to do with the battle of conflicting forces in the world, which the group brought in with them?

Could it be in some curious way prophetic of the need for protection of the ark—the flood waters were very churned up and the rain-drenched garden seemed significant; but there was behind all the wonderful sense of steadiness and protection and that all was within the palm of God's hand.

This is an interesting meditation. The snake or serpent is the symbol of kundalini, the creative power in the soul, sometimes called the great Mother. It is a twofold power comprising both good and evil, and it will stimulate and bring to activity either the positive or the negative force. It will stimulate the good in the soul and bring beauty, peace and happiness, or it might stimulate negative qualities in the soul and increase the bad qualities and the bad aspects, according to which predominate in the person. This is why it is considered dangerous to arouse it. It is also symbolised by the caduceus, the rod of Mercury—the higher and the lower mind entwined.

The symbol of the cross within the circle is that of the ancient Brotherhood and is all powerful in its protection against the darkness.

If the soul is under the control of the divine spirit, all the afflictions of the earthly life can have no power to disturb the reality of the peace deep within. The ark is the symbol of the holy place wherein the heavenly treasures are preserved.

I became aware of the mountain heights, the brothers, and the Star chamber of the golden temple. The aspiration to love filled me. This was the initiation of renunciation, the giving up of everything, all human ties and human love had to be renounced, for the love of God. When all human desire had been replaced by utter and complete surrender and we entered into the very centre and heart of the blazing jewel we found everything and everyone whom we had willingly and voluntarily renounced. All that was of God in them was intensified and amplified so that even the human love was more complete, more satisfying.

This is the lesson of desirelessness or surrender of the little will to the will of God. It is a hard lesson, but it must be learnt, not only theoretically but in complete acceptance of the events of everyday life. It can be summed up in the simple phrase, 'God knows best,' but we humans cannot accept this—we think *we* know best. Here also arises the question as to whether it is right to accept what appears to us to be evil, and whether or not we should fight against it. I think the Master gave the answer when he said, 'Resist not evil . . . but overcome evil with good.' So we come back to the wisdom of acceptance of God's will and the surrender of one's own judgment to the divine plan.

Whilst the lovely music was being played, I watched the six-pointed Star taking shape above our heads. This grew in light and beauty until it merged into the shape of the white wings of the eagle. We were all within the wings, outspread above the whole group, and I felt very emotional, but so unworthy of this.

Now I was shown a half-opened, golden rose, and I could see sunlight shining through it. The rose opened and grew large enough for me to enter its heart. I found myself on a high, flat place above earth, and we watched as the Brothers of the White Light formed a circle. They turned their faces towards the outer world, and lifted their hands upwards and outwards. Each hand touched that of his brother, and light streamed out from their fingers. It seemed a prayer of thanksgiving and praise, and was a wonderful sight.

My teacher now took me to a place which seemed halfway up a mountain. We stopped before some hut-like buildings, like large dog-kennels, and the doors of all the huts were standing wide-open. It was as black as pitch inside and I wasn't keen to enter, as I have been afraid of total darkness as long as I can remember. I made as if to turn away, then looked up into the face of my teacher as he stood beside me in his purple robe, all loving compassion. I turned back to the dark door-way and soon found myself inside. I recall clenching my hands in fear as I tried to see. Then I remembered—that as we had stood outside, I had seen a small window above the door. This didn't let in any light, yet the light had been shining *from the inside*. I began to think about this—and the thought came that out of the darkness came Light—that even in the deepest dark, light can shine forth. Darkness is only ignorance—seek and ye shall find. As this thought took root, all fear subsided. I really knew now that nothing could ever harm me, only the shell could be hurt, but *I* am indestructible. I am now, and ever will be. I was filled with joy beyond words.

Then your voice called me gently into a garden, and beside a lily-pond. All was peace, and there was an image of Buddha, carved in gold. The sun was shining and there were young saplings there. Suddenly, great flames came rushing towards me. I stayed where I was, knowing now that I could not be harmed, and the flames roared over me, leaving everything blackened. I was smiling, for this seemed proof to me that I was indestructible. Then I saw the teacher beside me, the sun shining upon his white hair and gentle features. He took me by the hand and showed me a flame. It was not a candle, but an oval flame made of the most beautiful violet light. This flame was a Being whose arms were uplifted in blessing and love. It was so very wonderful to behold, and I was filled with a yearning to gather the sick people into my arms and bring them into this glorious Presence to be healed and given knowledge.

Then from this wondrous flame came the simple words, 'Feed my sheep.' I was reluctant to return to the now unreal world of earth.

This peace and calm have stayed with me since last evening and I pray that in time I may be strong enough to build this into my make-up.

This meditation is another example of one of the truths which dawn in the soul through

meditation—that 'I', the spirit am indestructible and have nothing to fear. It also shows
how meditation can affect the daily life of the
aspirant.

    ▒ I was told to lean on the Master's heart,
which was soft, like rose petals, because it was
the rose. I could feel the exquisite softness
and then we were told we were with the Lord
Christ and leaning against his heart—and
I was so happy because I was already there.

This illustrates the development of the inner
sense of feeling and of touch. Another experience of the sense of feeling in meditation is
going to a blue lake and being invited to enter
it to bathe. The meditator is aware of the coolness of the water and has an exhilarating feeling
of being cleansed, healed and refreshed. All
aches and pains in the physical body seem to be
washed away in these healing waters. It is of
course the soul, in which the disease first
lodges, that is being cleansed, and so the physical body is relaxed and restored.

    ▒ I found I was on the tip of a golden pyra-
mid. Another one came down and pierced
it point downwards, and the whole became
a diamond, glowing with different coloured
lights from each facet. There was a golden
triangle next to the pyramid and the diamond
somehow balanced on its peak. At the foot
of the triangle was a plot of green grass and

in its centre a square pool of still and transparent clear water on which floated a lotus of heavenly blue. The sky was a very clear blue and across it the planets wheeled in their stately dance each radiating and intermingling their own colour rays. It was all very vivid and clear cut.

The words I hear as I read this meditation are: 'God's in His heaven, all's right with the world.' We enter heaven by a process of adjustment and balance, and when we have achieved this degree of divine wisdom we are at peace, we have learnt to surrender to the divine will because we know that God holds all life in His heart.

The varying coloured rays signify the different masters or adepts who are united in the one God-consciousness, and are all working to help humanity along the path of spiritual evolution.

The following very clearly detailed meditation gives an insight into the meaning of the pyramid and the six-pointed star.

By the lily pool a tall figure in a white robe came up to me. He took my hand and led me through a narrow tunnelway. At the end we came into a new world, full of bright yellow light. He led me up to a long stone stairway which I realised was the stairway into a pyramid. He walked in front of me and I had an opportunity to observe closely what he was wearing. It was a white robe, embroidered round the edges with gold in symbols—triangles, squares, cubes, circles and other geometric figures. He had a gold girdle and gold sandals. He had a white cloak around his shoulders which was also embroidered in gold with geometric symbols. He had brown, almost fair hair, quite long.

The room we entered was quite large; bookcases lined the righthand wall, and there were a number of screens, like flat televisions, on the lefthand wall. In the middle of the room were tables and chairs. My companion went to one of the bookshelves and brought out a large leatherbound book. It was closed with a gold clasp. He gave me a gold key and told me to unlock the book. I could not really comprehend what was in the book, but I thought it was an account with diagrams and pictures of the Atlantean civilisation. My companion then turned to the 'television' screens and turned one on. A film appeared—again I think of a part of Atlantis. It seemed to be a very modern city, yet dominated by a vast pyramid! It was not very clear—but I think my companion was either giving me knowledge of the Atlanteans or showing me a past incarnation.

We then left this room and went up many winding stairs to a room at the top of the pyramid. There were many white-robed people, and several officiants clothed in white and gold, as was my companion. I joined the other people—my companion joined the officiants. I realised it was a brotherhood meeting for we were perambulating round the room. . . . I noticed that the ceiling of the room was in fact the top of the pyramid and the very apex was not covered in—it was open to the sky—and through this opening poured the light of a glorious, pulsating golden star. As I looked at the star we all seemed to be caught up in a wave of light and became a pyramid of light. A corresponding pyramid came down from heaven and we were all in the centre of a pulsating three-dimensional six-pointed star. It was the most wonderful, exalting feeling.

I was already standing at the entrance to a cave knowing that I should soon enter it when I heard your voice describing it. As I moved forward I looked back over my shoulder and became aware of the light shining on the walls. The cave widened and I thought it had become a cathedral with stained-glass windows. This was the effect given by the light on the many coloured jewels you told us studded the walls. I went forward confidently and found the arched doorway. There was great joy there and singing and figures in white I presumed were choristers. The pass-word 'love' was with me, also 'sincerity.' The temple was, I knew, beautiful beyond words. In the centre was a square golden altar, which emitted a wondrous light. As I watched, this glow ascended and widened until shafts of light were formed like searchlight beams, raying outwards to the whole of creation. One was so conscious of the presence of the Master for there was such peace. I then seemed to be looking down on vast gardens laid out in a formal style, and could see the colourful designs laid out in flowers and low shrubs with pathways between trees and fountains —rather like the grounds of a palace. The grounds were full of happy people walking there. When the time came for me to return I entered the cave backwards facing where I had been. As I descended into the cave the light at the entrance became a shaft of light. As I returned slowly to earth conditions I knew the Master was with us all, and I heard him say, 'I will enfold you in my cloak' and I knew he had done so. I felt it being wrapped around me.

The Christ descended from his throne and took the chalice from the altar and the bread, and made the full circle of the brethren giving to each the wafer and the wine; and as each brother received he knelt and prayed and each prayer rose up like incense, and gradually built above the altar a purple covering like a canopy of cloud. When all had partaken the Christ ascended to the throne again and drank from the cup to show that all were one with Him. Then He set down the cup and sat upon the throne, and all fell again to meditation for a space and from a far inner archway came a procession of other brothers wearing long cloaks, and each carrying a pilgrim's cross. They made a semicircle before the throne, and the Christ rose and gave them a silent blessing, and the whole atmosphere pulsated with the power put forth. Then the pilgrim brothers rose and went in procession down the steep path by which we had ascended, to work in the world yet keeping direct contact with the temple and the Christ.

I have used this lovely account as the climax to these meditations, and it is self-explanatory. And now, I close this book with a meditation given to us by White Eagle:

'Now, let us all in humble spirit use our imagination and rise through the mists surrounding the earth . . . above the clouds and the mists you see the blue, blue sky and the sunlight. Go into that world, the world of flowers, an infinite and eternal garden, nature's manifestation of beauty and love. . .

'Now feel the peace . . . inhale the perfume of this heavenly garden. See the brethren clothed in simple white raiment walking these turfed paths, these smooth green paths. See the brethren walking with arms folded, their faces touched by a heavenly light. As you draw close to them, they smile at you and bow their heads in recognition and give you their blessing.

'See the angels whom you are told to follow

into the temple of the universal brotherhood. See there the innumerable shining spirits, all brethren in the Great White Light, their faces shining with the joy of life, for they are assembled to worship and give thanks to their heavenly Father and holy Mother. All heads are bowed and rays of light are seen issuing from the heart centre of every soul in this assembly.

'The temple is built of mother-of-pearl, built of the pearl ray and formed like a shell, perfect, glistening with the light and colour of mother-of-pearl. It expands into limitless space.

'In the heart of the temple is the Lord Christ, the Sun, the Sun of life, the Son of God, who is all love. We see Him in human form, the manifestation of pure love. He smiles upon you and his hands are raised in blessing. "Lo! I am with you always. . ."

'Feel the power pulsating through you, you are at one with IT, with the cosmic life and consciousness . . . you are one with all you love. All are part of you, and you are part of God.

'We leave you in silent worship in this temple of universal brotherhood.'